D. H. Lawrence

Selected Poems

*

Edited by Dr Jan Todd

Oxford University Press
1993

Oxford University Press, Walton Street, Oxford OX2 6DP

Oxford New York Toronto
Delhi Bombay Calcutta Madras Karachi
Kuala Lumpur Singapore Hong Kong Tokyo
Nairobi Dar es Salaam Cape Town
Melbourne Auckland Madrid

and associated companies in
Berlin Ibadan

First published by Oxford University Press

ISBN 0 19 831962 2

Typeset by Pentacor PLC, High Wycombe, Bucks
Printed and bound in Great Britain by
Butler & Tanner Ltd, Frome and London

The publishers would like to thank the following for permission to
reproduce photographs:

Hulton Deutsch Collection Ltd p.179; Nottingham University
Library, p.180; Nottinghamshire County Council p.177, p.178 a),
p.178b; University of Texas of Austin, Harry Ransom Humanities
Research Centre p.181.

The cover illustration is by Susan Scott

Contents

Acknowledgements *vi*

Editors *vi*

Foreword *vii*

The Poems
from *Early Poems*
Discord in Childhood *1*
Piano *1*
The Wild Common *2*
Cherry Robbers *4*
Cruelty and Love *4*
A Collier's Wife *6*
Violets *8*
End of Another Home-Holiday *10*
After the Opera *12*
The Bride *13*
Sorrow *13*
Whether or Not *14*
A Winter's Tale *22*
Ballad of Another Ophelia *22*
The Chief Mystery *24*

from *Look! We Have Come Through!*
Bei Hennef *26*
A Young Wife *27*
Gloire de Dijon *28*
Roses on the Breakfast Table *28*
Meeting Among the Mountains *29*
Giorno Dei Morti *30*
Song of a Man Who Has Come Through *31*
Craving for Spring *32*

from *Birds, Beasts and Flowers*
Peach   37
Medlars and Sorb-Apples   38
Almond Blossom   40
The Mosquito   44
Fish   47
Man and Bat   53
Snake   59
Baby Tortoise   62
Tortoise Shout   65
Turkey-Cock   69
Humming-Bird   72
Kangaroo   73
Mountain Lion   76

from *Pansies*
How Beastly the Bourgeois Is   78
When I Went to the Circus   79
Whatever Man Makes   82
Good Husbands Make Unhappy Wives   82
The Elephant is Slow to Mate   82
The Mess of Love   83
Red-Herring   84
Riches   85
To Women, as Far as I'm Concerned   85
Desire is Dead   86
Wages   86
Relativity   87
The Triumph of the Machine   87
For a Moment   89
Thought   90

from *Last Poems*
Middle of the World   91
Red Geranium and Godly Mignonette   92
The Man of Tyre   93
Whales Weep Not!   94

Invocation to the Moon   96
Bavarian Gentians   97
In the Cities   98
The Ship of Death   99
Shadows   103

Notes   105
from *Early Poems*   105
from *Look! We Have Come Through!*   112
from *Birds, Beasts and Flowers*   116
from *Pansies*   125
from *Last Poems*   129

Approaches   135
Approaches through Poetic Form   135
  Metre and Free Verse   136
  Early Poems: The Young Man and the Demon   138
  Look! We Have Come Through!: Poetry of the
    Immediate Present   142
  Birds, Beasts and Flowers: Acts of Attention   145
  Pansies: Fresh Air of Open Consciousness   149
Approaches Through Lawrence's Life   150
Approaches Through Lawrence's Ideas   154
  Religion   154
  Sex   156
  Thinking   160
  Symbol and Myth   161
Approaches Through the Single Poem   162
  Bavarian Gentians   162

Chronology   167

Further Reading   170

Tasks   172

Illustrations   177

Index of Titles and First Lines   182

Acknowledgements

I would like to thank Dr Victor Lee, Lucy Hooper, and Penny Todd for their help in preparing this edition, and Peter Roberts for my first opportunity to read and discuss Lawrence's poems.

The poems in this edition are drawn from two main sources. The *Early Poems* come from Keith Sagar's *Selected Poems*, while the others come from the two-volume *Complete Poems* edited by Vivian de Sola Pinto and Warren Roberts. The editor and publisher would like to thank Laurence Pollinger Ltd and the Estate of Frieda Lawrence Ravagli for their permission to use A *Winter's Tale* in this edition.

Editors

Dr Victor Lee

Victor Lee, the series editor, read English at University College, Cardiff. He was later awarded his doctorate at the University of Oxford. He has taught at secondary and tertiary level, and is currently working at the Open University. There, he has been involved in the making of a considerable number of texts, television and radio programmes. Victor Lee's experience as an examiner is very wide: he has been a Chief Examiner in English at A-level for three different boards stretching over a period of twenty years.

Dr Jan Todd

Jan Todd read English at Jesus College, Cambridge and took a D. Phil. at the University of York. He has worked as a teacher and examiner in secondary and higher education and is currently Head of English at Haywards Heath College.

Foreword

Oxford Student Texts are specifically aimed at presenting poetry and drama to an audience which is studying English Literature at an advanced level. Each text is designed as an integrated whole consisting of three main parts. The poetry or the play is always placed first to stress its importance and to encourage students to enjoy it without secondary critical material of any kind. When help is needed on other occasions, the second and third parts of these texts, the Notes and the Approaches, provide it.

The Notes perform two functions. First, they provide information and explain allusions. Secondly, and this is where they differ from most texts at this level, they often raise questions of central concern to the interpretation of the poem or the play being dealt with, particularly in the use of a general note placed at the beginning of the particular notes.

The third part, the Approaches section, deals with major issues of response to the particular selection of poetry or drama, as opposed to the work of the writer as a whole. One of the major aims of this part of the text is to emphasize that there is no one right answer to interpretation, but a series of approaches. Readers are given guidance as to what counts as evidence, but, in the end, left to make up their mind as to which are the most suitable interpretations, or to add their own.

To help achieve this, the Approaches section contains a number of activity-discussion sequences, although it must be stressed that these are optional. Significant issues about the poetry or the play are raised in these activities. Readers are invited to tackle these activities before proceeding to the discussion section where possible responses to the questions raised in the activities are considered. Their main function is to engage readers actively in the ideas of the text. However, these activity-discussion sequences are so arranged that, if readers wish to treat the Approaches as continuous prose and not attempt the activities, they can.

At the end of each text there is also a list of Tasks. Whereas the activity-discussion sequences are aimed at increasing understanding of the literary work itself, these tasks are intended to help explore ideas about the poetry or the play after the student has completed the reading of the work and the studying of the Notes and Approaches. These tasks are particularly helpful for coursework projects or in preparing for an examination.

Victor Lee   Series Editor

The Poems

from *Early Poems*

Discord in Childhood

Outside the house an ash-tree hung its terrible whips,
And at night when the wind arose, the lash of the tree
Shrieked and slashed the wind, as a ship's
Weird rigging in a storm shrieks hideously.

Within the house two voices arose in anger, a slender
    lash
Whistling delirious rage, and the dreadful sound
Of a thick lash booming and bruising, until it drowned
The other voice in a silence of blood, 'neath the noise of
    the ash.

Piano

Softly, in the dusk, a woman is singing to me;
Taking me back down the vista of years, till I see
A child sitting under the piano, in the boom of the
    tingling strings
And pressing the small, poised feet of a mother who
    smiles as she sings.

In spite of myself, the insidious mastery of song
Betrays me back, till the heart of me weeps to belong
To the old Sunday evenings at home, with winter outside
And hymns in the cosy parlour, the tinkling piano our
    guide.

So now it is vain for the singer to burst into clamour
10 With the great black piano appassionato. The glamour
Of childish days is upon me, my manhood is cast
Down in the flood of remembrance, I weep like a child
    for the past.

The Wild Common

The quick sparks on the gorse bushes are leaping,
Little jets of sunlight-texture imitating flame;
Above them, exultant, the peewits are sweeping:
They are lords of the desolate wastes of sadness their
    screamings proclaim.

Rabbits, handfuls of brown earth, lie
Low-rounded on the mournful grass they have bitten
    down to the quick.
Are they asleep? – Are they alive? – Now see, when I
Move my arms the hill bursts and heaves under their
    spurting kick.

The common flaunts bravely; but below, from the rushes
10 Crowds of glittering king-cups surge to challenge the
    blossoming bushes;
There the lazy streamlet pushes
Its curious course mildly; here it wakes again, leaps,
    laughs, and gushes

Into a deep pond, an old sheep-dip,
Dark, overgrown with willows, cool, with the brook
    ebbing through so slow;
Naked on the steep, soft lip
Of the bank I stand watching my own white shadow
    quivering to and fro.

What if the gorse flowers shrivelled and kissing were
    lost?
Without the pulsing waters, where were the marigolds
    and the songs of the brook?
If my veins and my breasts with love embossed
20   Withered, my insolent soul would be gone like flowers
    that the hot wind took.

So my soul like a passionate woman turns,
Filled with remorseful terror to the man she scorned,
    and her love
For myself in my own eyes' laughter burns,
Runs ecstatic over the pliant folds rippling down to my
    belly from the breast-lights above.

Over my sunlit skin the warm, clinging air,
Rich with the songs of seven larks singing at once, goes
    kissing me glad.
And the soul of the wind and my blood compare
Their wandering happiness, and the wind, wasted in
    liberty, drifts on and is sad.

Oh but the water loves me and folds me,
30   Plays with me, sways me, lifts me and sinks me as though
    it were living blood,
Blood of a heaving woman who holds me,
Owning my supple body a rare glad thing, supremely
    good.

Cherry Robbers

Under the long, dark boughs, like jewels red
    In the hair of an Eastern girl
Shine strings of crimson cherries, as if had bled
    Blood-drops beneath each curl.

Under the glistening cherries, with folded wings
    Three dead birds lie:
Pale-breasted throstles and a blackbird, robberlings
    Stained with red dye.

Under the haystack a girl stands laughing at me,
10   With cherries hung round her ears—
Offering me her scarlet fruit: I will see
    If she has any tears.

Cruelty and Love

What large, dark hands are those at the window
Lifted, grasping the golden light
Which weaves its way through the creeper leaves
    To my heart's delight?

Ah, only the leaves! But in the west,
In the west I see a redness come
Over the evening's burning breast—
    —'Tis the wound of love goes home!

    The woodbine creeps abroad
10   Calling low to her lover:
        The sun-lit flirt who all the day
        Has poised above her lips in play
        And stolen kisses, shallow and gay
        Of pollen, now has gone away
        —She woos the moth with her sweet, low word,
    And when above her his broad wings hover

Then her bright breast she will uncover
And yield her honey-drop to her lover.

Into the yellow, evening glow
20 Saunters a man from the farm below,
Leans, and looks in at the low-built shed   *couplet*
Where hangs the swallow's marriage bed.
        The bird lies warm against the wall.
        She glances quick her startled eyes
        Towards him, then she turns away   *couplet*
        Her small head, making warm display   *over*
        Of red upon the throat. His terrors sway
        Her out of the nest's warm, busy ball,
        Whose plaintive cry is heard as she flies   *couplet.*
30   In one blue stoop from out the sties
        Into the evening's empty hall.

Oh, water-hen, beside the rushes   *Couplet*
Hide your quaint, unfading blushes,
Still your quick tail, and lie as dead,
Till the distance folds over his ominous tread.   *Couplet*

The rabbit presses her ears,
Turns back her liquid, anguished eyes
And crouches low: then with wild spring (
Spurts from the terror of *his* oncoming
40 To be choked back, the wire ring |
Her frantic effort throttling:

        Piteous brown ball of quivering fears!
        Ah soon in his large, hard hands she dies, __
        And swings all loose to the swing of his walk. |
        Yet calm and kindly are his eyes   __
        And ready to open in brown surprise
        Should I not answer to his talk   \
        Or should he my tears surmise.

I hear his hand on the latch, and rise from my chair
50   Watching the door open: he flashes bare
His strong teeth in a smile, and flashes his eyes
In a smile like triumph upon me; then careless-wise
He flings the rabbit soft on the table board
And comes towards me: ah, the uplifted sword
Of his hand against my bosom, and oh, the broad
Blade of his hand that raises my face to applaud
His coming: he raises up my face to him
And caresses my mouth with his fingers, which still
     smell grim
Of the rabbit's fur! God, I am caught in a snare!
60   I know not what fine wire is round my throat,
I only know I let him finger there
My pulse of life, letting him nose like a stoat
Who sniffs with joy before he drinks the blood:
And down his mouth comes to my mouth, and down
His dark bright eyes descend like a fiery hood
Upon my mind: his mouth meets mine, and a flood
Of sweet fire sweeps across me, so I drown
Within him, die, and find death good.

A Collier's Wife

Somebody's knocking at the door
     Mother, come down and see.
—I's think it's nobbut a beggar,
     Say, I'm busy.

It's not a beggar, mother, —hark
     How hard he knocks...
—Eh, tha'rt a mard-'arsed kid,
     'E'll gi'e thee socks!

Shout an' ax what 'e wants,
10   I canna come down.
—'E says 'Is it Arthur Holliday's?'
     Say 'Yes,' tha clown.

'E says, 'Tell your mother as 'er mester's
     Got hurt i' th' pit.'
What – oh my sirs, 'e never says that,
     That's niver it.

Come out o' the way an' let me see,
     Eh, there's no peace!
An' stop thy scraightin', childt,
20   Do shut thy face.

'Your mester's 'ad an accident,
     An' they're ta'ein 'im i' th' ambulance
To Nottingham,' – Eh dear o' me
     If 'e's not a man for mischance!

Wheers he hurt this time, lad?
     – I dunna know,
They on'y towd me it wor bad –
     It would be so!

Eh, what a man! – an' that cobbly road,
30   They'll jolt him a'most to death,
I'm sure he's in for some trouble
     Nigh every time he takes breath.

Out o' my way, childt – dear o' me, wheer
     Have I put his clean stockings and shirt;
Goodness knows if they'll be able
     To take off his pit dirt.

An' what a moan he'll make – there niver
     Was such a man for a fuss

If anything ailed him – at any rate
40   *I* shan't have him to nuss.

I do hope it's not very bad!
    Eh, what a shame it seems
As some should ha'e hardly a smite o' trouble
    An' others has reams.

It's a shame as 'e should be knocked about
    Like this, I'm sure it is!
He's had twenty accidents, if he's had one;
    Owt bad, an' it's his.

There's one thing, we'll have peace for a bit,
50   Thank Heaven for a peaceful house;
An' there's compensation, sin' it's accident,
    An' club money – I nedn't grouse.

An' a fork an' a spoon he'll want, an' what else;
    I s'll never catch that train –
What a traipse it is if a man gets hurt –
    I s'd think he'll get right again.

Violets

Sister, tha knows while we was on the planks
    Aside o' th' grave, while th' coffin wor lyin' yet
On th' yaller clay, an' white flowers top of it
    Tryin' to keep off 'n him a bit o' th' wet,

An' parson makin' haste, an' a' the black
    Huddlin' close together a cause o' th' rain,
Did t' 'appen ter notice a bit of a lass away back
    By a head-stun, sobbin' an' sobbin' again?

    —How should I be lookin' round
10   An' me standin' on the plank

Beside the open ground,
Where our Ted 'ud soon be sank?

Yi, an' 'im that young,
Snapped sudden out of all
His wickedness, among
Pals worse n'r ony name as you could call.

Let be that; there's some o' th' bad as we
Like better nor all your good, an' 'e was one.
—An' cos I liked him best, yi, bett'r nor thee,
20   I canna bide to think where he is gone.

Ah know tha liked 'im bett'r nor me. But let
Me tell thee about this lass. When you had gone
Ah stopped behind on t' pad i' th' drippin wet
An' watched what 'er 'ad on.

Tha should ha' seed 'er slive up when we'd gone,
Tha should ha' seed her kneel an' look in
At th' sloppy wet grave – an' 'er little neck shone
That white, an' 'er shook that much, I'd like to begin

Scraightin' mysen as well. 'Er undid 'er black
30   Jacket at th' bosom, an' took from out of it
Over a double 'andful of violets, all in a pack
Ravelled blue and white – warm, for a bit

O' th' smell come waftin' to me. 'Er put 'er face
Right intil 'em and scraighted out again,
Then after a bit 'er dropped 'em down that place,
An' I come away, because o' the teemin' rain.

End of Another Home-Holiday

1

When shall I see the half moon sink again
Behind the black sycamore at the end of the garden?
When will the scent of the dim, white phlox
Creep up the wall to me, and in at my open window?

Why is it, the long slow stroke of the midnight bell,
    (Will it never finish the twelve?)
Falls again and again on my heart with a heavy
    reproach?

The moon-mist is over the village, out of the mist speaks
    the bell,
And all the little roofs of the village bow low, pitiful,
    beseeching, resigned:
10   Oh, little home, what is it I have not done well?

Ah home, suddenly I love you,
As I hear the sharp clean trot of a pony down the road,
Succeeding sharp little sounds dropping into the silence,
Clear upon the long-drawn hoarseness of a train across
    the valley.

The light has gone out from under my mother's door.
        That she should love me so,
        She, so lonely, greying now,
        And I leaving her,
        Bent on my pursuits!

20   Love is the great Asker,
      The sun and the rain do not ask the secret
      Of the time when the grain struggles down in the
        dark.
      The moon walks her lonely way without anguish,
      Because no loved one grieves over her departure.

2

Forever, ever by my shoulder pitiful Love will linger,
Crouching as little houses crouch under the mist when I
turn.
Forever, out of the mist the church lifts up her
reproachful finger,
Pointing my eyes in wretched defiance where love hides
her face to mourn.

Oh but the rain creeps down to wet the grain
30   That struggles alone in the dark,
And asking nothing, cheerfully steals back again!

The moon sets forth o'nights
To walk the lonely, dusky heights
Serenely, with steps unswerving;
Pursued by no sigh of bereavement,
No tears of love unnerving
Her constant tread:
While ever at my side,
Frail and sad, with grey bowed head,
40   The beggar-woman, the yearning-eyed
Inexorable love goes lagging.

The wild young heifer, glancing distraught,
With a strange new knocking of life at her side
Runs seeking a loneliness.
The little grain draws down the earth to hide.
Nay, even the slumberous egg, as it labours under the
shell,
Patiently to divide, and self-divide,
Asks to be hidden, and wishes nothing to tell.

But when I draw the scanty cloak of silence over my eyes,
50   Piteous Love comes peering under the hood.
Touches the clasp with trembling fingers, and tries

To put her ear to the painful sob of my blood,
While her tears soak through to my breast,
>   Where they burn and cauterize.

3

The moon lies back and reddens.
In the valley, a corncrake calls
>   Monotonously,
With a piteous, unalterable plaint, that deadens
>   My confident activity:
60   With a hoarse, insistent request that falls
>   Unweariedly, unweariedly,
>   Asking something more of me,
>   Yet more of me!

After the Opera

Down the stone stairs
Girls with their large eyes wide with tragedy
Lift looks of shocked and momentous emotions up at me.
And I smile.

Ladies
Stepping like birds with their bright and pointed feet
Peer anxiously forth, as if for a boat to carry them out of
>   the wreckage,
And among the wreck of the theatre crowd
I stand and smile.

10   They take tragedy so becomingly.
Which pleases me.

But when I meet the weary eyes
The reddened aching eyes of the bar-man with thin arms,
I am glad to go back where I came from.

The Bride

My love looks like a girl to-night,
    But she is old.
The plaits that lie along her pillow
    Are not gold,
But threaded with filigree silver,
And uncanny cold.

She looks like a young maiden, since her brow
    Is smooth and fair,
Her cheeks are very smooth, her eyes are closed.
10   She sleeps a rare
Still winsome sleep, so still, and so composed.

Nay, but she sleeps like a bride, and dreams her dreams
    Of perfect things.
She lies at last, the darling, in the shape of her dream,
    And her dead mouth sings
By its shape, like the thrushes in clear evenings.

Sorrow

Why does the thin grey strand
Floating up from the forgotten
Cigarette between my fingers,
Why does it trouble me?

Ah, you will understand;
When I carried my mother downstairs,
A few times only, at the beginning
Of her soft-foot malady,

I should find, for a reprimand
10 To my gaiety, a few long grey hairs
On the breast of my coat; and one by one
I watched them float up the dark chimney.

Whether or Not

1

Dunna thee tell me it's his'n, mother,
   Dunna thee, dunna thee.
—Oh ay! he'll be comin' to tell thee his-sèn
   Wench, wunna he?

Tha doesna mean to say to me, mother,
   He's gone wi that—
—My gel, owt'll do for a man i' the dark,
   Tha's got it flat.

But 'er's old, mother, 'er's twenty year
10   Older nor him—
—Ay, an' yaller as a crowflower, an' yet i' the dark
   Er'd do for Tim.

Tha niver believes it, mother, does ter?
   It's somebody's lies.
—Ax him thy-sèn wench – a widder's lodger;
   It's no surprise.

2

A widow of forty-five
With a bitter, swarthy skin,
To ha' 'ticed a lad o' twenty-five
20   An' 'im to have been took in!

A widow of forty-five
As has sludged like a horse all her life,

Till 'er's tough as whit-leather, to slive
Atween a lad an' 'is wife!

A widow of forty-five,
A tough old otchel wi' long
Witch teeth, an' 'er black hawk-eyes as I've
Mistrusted all along!

An' me as 'as kep my-sen
30   Shut like a daisy bud,
Clean an' new an' nice, so's when
He wed he'd ha'e summat good!

An' 'im as nice an' fresh
As any man i' the force,
To ha'e gone an' given his white young flesh
To a woman that coarse!

3

You're stout to brave this snow, Miss Stainwright,
   Are you makin' Brinsley way?
—I'm off up th' line to Underwood
40   Wi' a dress as is wanted to-day.

Oh are you goin' to Underwood?
   'Appen then you've 'eered?
—What's that as 'appen I've 'eered-on, Missis,
   Speak up, you nedna be feared.

Why, your young man an' Widow Naylor,
   Her as he lodges wi',
They say he's got her wi' childt; but there,
   It's nothing to do wi' me.

Though if it's true they'll turn him out
50   O' th' p'lice force, without fail;
An' if it's not true, I'd back my life
   They'll listen to *her* tale.

Well, I'm believin' no tale, Missis,
    I'm seein' for my-sen;
An' when I know for sure, Missis,
    I'll talk *then*.

4

Nay robin red-breast, tha nedna
    Sit noddin' thy head at me;
My breast's as red as thine, I reckon
60   Flayed red, if tha could but see.

Nay, you blessed pee-whips,
    You nedna screet at me!
I'm screetin' my-sen, but are-na goin'
    To let iv'rybody see.

Tha *art* smock-ravelled, bunny,
    Larropin' neck an' crop
I' th' snow: but I's warrant thee, bunny,
    I'm further ower th' top.

5

Now sithee theer at th' railroad crossin'
70   Warmin' his-sen at the stool o' fire
Under the tank as fills the ingines,
If there isn't my dearly-beloved liar!

My constable wi' 'is buttoned breast
As stout as the truth, my sirs! – An' 'is face
As bold as a robin! It's much he cares
For this nice old shame and disgrace.

Oh but he drops his flag when 'e sees me,
Yes, an' 'is face goes white... oh yes
Tha can stare at me wi' thy fierce blue eyes,
80   But tha doesna stare me out, I guess!

6

Whativer brings thee out so far
        In a' this depth o' snow?
—I'm takin' 'ome a weddin' dress
        If tha maun know.

Why, is there a weddin' at Underwood,
        As tha ne'd trudge up here?
—It's Widow Naylor's weddin'-dress,
        An' 'er's wantin it, I hear.

'Er doesna want no weddin-dress...
90   What – but what dost mean?
—Doesn't ter know what I mean, Tim? – Yi,
        Tha must 'a' been hard to wean!

Tha'rt a good-un at suckin-in yet, Timmy;
        But tell me, isn't it true
As 'er'll be wantin' *my* weddin' dress
        In a week or two?

Tha's no occasions ter ha'e me on
        Lizzie – what's done is done!
—*Done*, I should think so – Done! But might
100   I ask when tha begun?

It's thee as 'as done it as much as me,
        Lizzie, I tell thee that.
—'Me gotten a childt to thy landlady –!'
        Tha's gotten thy answer pat,

As tha allers hast – but let me tell thee
        Hasna ter sent me whoam, when I
Was a'most burstin' mad o' my-sen
        An' walkin' in agony;

After thy kisses, Lizzie, after
110   Tha's lain right up to me Lizzie, an' melted

Into me, melted into me, Lizzie,
    Till I was verily swelted.

An' if my landlady seed me like it,
    An' if 'er clawkin', tiger's eyes
Went through me just as the light went out
    Is it any cause for surprise?

No cause for surprise at all, my lad,
    After lickin' and snuffin' at me, tha could
Turn thy mouth on a woman like her—
120   Did ter find her good?

Ay, I did, but afterwards
    I should like to ha' killed her!
—Afterwards! – an' after how long
    Wor it tha'd like to 'a killed her?

Say no more, Liz, dunna thee,
    I might lose my-sen.
—I'll only say good-bye to thee, Timothy,
    An' gi'e her thee back again.

I'll ta'e they word 'Good-bye,' Liz,
130   But I shonna marry her,
I shonna for nobody. – It is
    Very nice on you, Sir.

The childt maun ta'e its luck, it maun,
    An' she maun ta'e *her* luck,
For I tell ye I shonna marry her–
    What her's got, her took.

That's spoken like a man, Timmy,
    That's spoken like a man...
'He up an' fired off his pistol
140   An' then away he ran.'

I damn well shanna marry 'er,
  So chew at it no more,
Or I'll chuck the flamin' lot of you—
  —You nedn't have swore.

7

That's his collar round the candle-stick
An' that's the dark blue tie I bought 'im,
An' these is the woman's kids he's so fond on,
An' 'ere comes the cat that caught 'im.

I dunno where his eyes was – a gret
150 Round-shouldered hag! My sirs, to think
Of him stoopin' to her! You'd wonder he could
Throw hisself in that sink.

I expect you know who I am, Mrs Naylor!
  —Who yer are? – yis, you're Lizzie Stainwright.
'An 'appen you might guess what I've come for?
  —'Appen I mightn't, 'appen I might.

You knowed as I was courtin' Tim Merfin.
  —Yis, I knowed 'e wor courtin' thee.
An' yet you've been carryin' on wi' him.
160   —Ay, an' 'im wi' me.

Well, now you've got to pay for it,
  —An' if I han, what's that to thee?
For 'e isn't goin' to marry you.
  —Is it a toss-up 'twixt thee an' me?

It's no toss-up 'twixt thee an' me.
  —Then what art colleyfoglin' for?
I'm not havin' your orts an' slarts.
  —Which on us said you wor?

I want you to know 'e's non *marryin'* you.
170   —Tha wants 'im thy-sen too bad.

Though I'll see as 'e pays you, an' comes to the scratch.
—Tha'rt for doin' a lot wi' th' lad.

8

To think I should ha'e to haffle an' caffle
    Wi' a woman, an' pay 'er a price
For lettin' me marry the lad as I thought
    To marry wi' cabs an' rice.

But we'll go unbeknown to the registrar,
    An' give *'er* what money there is,
For I won't be beholden to such as her
180   For anythink of his.

9

Take off thy duty stripes, Tim,
    An' come wi' me in here,
Ta'e off thy p'lice-man's helmet
    An' look me clear.

I wish tha hadna done it, Tim,
    I do, an' that I do!
For whenever I look thee i' th' face, I s'll see
    Her face too.

I wish tha could wesh 'er off'n thee,
190   For I used to think that thy
Face was the finest thing that iver
    Met my eye...

10

Twenty pound o' thy own tha hast, and fifty pound ha'e I,
Thine shall go to pay the woman, an' wi' my bit we'll buy
All as we shall want for furniture when tha leaves this
    place,
An' we'll be married at th' registrar – now lift thy face.

Lift thy face an' look at me, man, up an' look at me:
Sorry I am for this business, an' sorry if I ha'e driven
  thee
To such a thing: but it's a poor tale, that I'm bound to
  say,
200 Before I can ta'e thee I've got a widow of forty-five to
  pay.

Dunnat thee think but what I love thee – I love thee
  well,
But 'deed an' I wish as this tale o' thine wor niver my
  tale to tell;
Deed an' I wish as I could stood at the altar wi' thee an'
  been proud o' thee,
That I could ha' been first woman to thee, as thou'rt first
  man to me.

But we maun ma'e the best on't – I'll rear thy childt
  if'er'll yield it to me,
An' then wi' that twenty pound we gi'e 'er I s'd think 'er
  wunna be
So very much worser off than 'er wor before – An' now
  look up
An' answer me – for I've said my say, an' there's no more
  sorrow to sup.

Yi, tha'rt a man, tha'rt a fine man, but niver a baby had
  eyes
210 As sulky an' ormin' as thine. Hast owt to say otherwise
From what I've arranged wi' thee? Eh man, what a
  stubborn jackass thou art,
Kiss me then – there! – ne'er mind if I scraight – I wor
  fond o' thee, Sweetheart.

A Winter's Tale

Yesterday the fields were only grey with scattered snow,
And now the longest grass-leaves hardly emerge;
Yet her deep footsteps mark the snow, and go
On towards the pines at the hill's white verge.

I cannot see her, since the mist's pale scarf
Obscures the dark wood and the dull orange sky;
But she's waiting, I know, impatient and cold, half
Sobs struggling into her frosty sigh.

Why does she come so promptly, when she must know
10   She's only the nearer to the inevitable farewell?
The hill is steep, on the snow my steps are slow—
Why does she come, when she knows what I have to
      tell?

Ballad of Another Ophelia

Oh the green glimmer of apples in the orchard,
Lamps in a wash of rain!
Oh the wet walk of my brown hen through the
      stackyard,
Oh tears on the window pane!

Nothing now will ripen the bright green apples,
Full of disappointment and of rain,
Brackish they will taste, of tears, when the yellow
      dapples
Of autumn tell the withered tale again.

All round the yard it is cluck, my brown hen,
10   Cluck, and the rain-wet wings,
Cluck, my marigold bird, and again
Cluck for your yellow darlings.

For the grey rat found the gold thirteen
Huddled away in the dark:
Flutter for a moment, oh the best is quick and keen,
Extinct one yellow-fluffy spark.

Once I had a lover bright like running water,
Once his face was laughing like the sky;
Open like the sky looking down in all its laughter
20   On the buttercups, and the buttercups was I.

What, then, is there hidden in the skirts of all the
     blossom?
What is peeping from your wings, oh mother hen?
'Tis the sun who asks the question, in a lovely haste for
     wisdom;
What a lovely haste for wisdom is in men!

Yea, but it is cruel when undressed is all the blossom,
And her shift is lying white upon the floor,
That a grey one, like a shadow, like a rat, a thief, a rain-
     storm,
Creeps upon her then and gathers in his store.

Oh the grey garner that is full of half-grown apples,
30   Oh the golden sparkles laid extinct!
And oh, behind the cloud-sheaves, like yellow autumn
     dapples,
Did you see the wicked sun that winked!

The Chief Mystery

The stinging nettles on my wrists woke me,
  Who had not slept...
I do not know where I had been
Nor what had become of me
  But I had not slept...
I only know that like a sod
In a meadow lost I lay,
And that a peewit called...
  But whether it called in my soul,
10   Or whether it rang in the air,
  Or whether my heart was its nest,
   I do not know.
I was there, that was all...
And like a sod in a meadow
I was embedded in the rest of things
Along with the moon.
  For the full moon shone; but whether
  It lay on me as on water,
  Or whether I was the darkness with arched wings
20   Hovering over it
  To fold in a shining concave the pale night,
   I do not know.
I awoke with the young nettles on my wrists,
  And I lifted my head;
And then I knew I had taken my mouth from her throat
  And I raised my breast;
Knowing then I had taken my bosom from her crushed
  breasts.
  And I went back with my mouth to her mouth
  So glad to have been lost,
30   So glad to find myself again.

Yet looking again at the night
Still I could not distinguish myself:
I said 'This is grass that twinkles in the dark,
    There is something about that they call the wind,
    And that white scud of heaven
    Is a track of clouds across the moon;
    But I, where among them all am I?'

Then the stinging nettles on my wrists
Showed me some other lovers stealing down the other
    hedgerow,
40   And I lay close down,
Saying 'It is she – it is I –
That is her small ear against my eyes,
This is I – this is I –

Perhaps the tiny young nettles have stung her ears.'
And I took her ear like the leaf of a water-flower
    between my lips,
And I said 'Love?'
For I was not sure of myself.
But she put her fingers on my neck, under my collar,
And her fingers were cool,
50   And I said, ''Tis I,
I am here!'

from
Look! We Have Come Through!

Bei Hennef

The little river twittering in the twilight,
The wan, wondering look of the pale sky,
    This is almost bliss.

And everything shut up and gone to sleep,
All the troubles and anxieties and pain
    Gone under the twilight.

Only the twilight now, and the soft 'Sh!' of the river
    That will last for ever.

And at last I know my love for you is here;
10 I can see it all, it is whole like the twilight,
It is large, so large, I could not see it before,
Because of the little lights and flickers and interruptions,
    Troubles, anxieties and pains.

    You are the call and I am the answer,
    You are the wish, and I the fulfilment,
    You are the night, and I the day.
        What else? it is perfect enough.
        It is perfectly complete,
        You and I,
20   What more—?

Strange, how we suffer in spite of this!

Hennef am Rhein

A Young Wife

The pain of loving you
Is almost more than I can bear.

I walk in fear of you.
The darkness starts up where
You stand, and the night comes through
Your eyes when you look at me.

Ah never before did I see
The shadows that live in the sun!

Now every tall glad tree
10 Turns round its back to the sun
And looks down on the ground, to see
The shadow it used to shun.

At the foot of each glowing thing
A night lies looking up.

Oh, and I want to sing
And dance, but I can't lift up
My eyes from the shadows: dark
They lie spilt round the cup.

What is it?—Hark
20 The faint fine seethe in the air!

Like the seething sound in a shell!
It is death still seething where
The wild-flower shakes its bell
And the skylark twinkles blue—

The pain of loving you
Is almost more than I can bear.

Gloire de Dijon

When she rises in the morning
I linger to watch her;
She spreads the bath-cloth underneath the window
And the sunbeams catch her
Glistening white on the shoulders,
While down her sides the mellow
Golden shadow glows as
She stoops to the sponge, and her swung breasts
Sway like full-blown yellow
10   Gloire de Dijon roses.

She drips herself with water, and her shoulders
Glisten as silver, they crumple up
Like wet and falling roses, and I listen
For the sluicing of their rain-dishevelled petals.
In the window full of sunlight
Concentrates her golden shadow
Fold on fold, until it glows as
Mellow as the glory roses.

Icking

Roses on the Breakfast Table

Just a few of the roses we gathered from the Isar
Are fallen, and their mauve-red petals on the cloth
Float like boats on a river, while other
Roses are ready to fall, reluctant and loth.

She laughs at me across the table, saying
I am beautiful. I look at the rumpled young roses
And suddenly realize, in them as in me,
How lovely is the self this day discloses.

Meeting Among the Mountains

The little pansies by the road have turned
Away their purple faces and their gold,
And evening has taken all the bees from the thyme,
And all the scent is shed away by the cold.

Against the hard and pale blue evening sky
The mountain's new-dropped summer snow is clear
Glistening in steadfast stillness: like transcendent
Clean pain sending on us a chill down here.

Christ on the Cross! – his beautiful young man's body
10 Has fallen dead upon the nails, and hangs
White and loose at last, with all the pain
Drawn on his mouth, eyes broken at last by his pangs.

And slowly down the mountain road, belated,
A bullock wagon comes; so I am ashamed
To gaze any more at the Christ, whom the mountain
    snows
Whitely confront; I wait on the grass, am lamed.

The breath of the bullock stains the hard, chill air,
The band is across its brow, and it scarcely seems
To draw the load, so still and slow it moves,
20 While the driver on the shaft sits crouched in dreams.

Surely about his sunburnt face is something
That vexes me with wonder. He sits so still
Here among all this silence, crouching forward,
Dreaming and letting the bullock take its will.

I stand aside on the grass to let them go;
—And Christ, I have met his accusing eyes again,
The brown eyes black with misery and hate, that look
Full in my own, and the torment starts again.

One moment the hate leaps at me standing there,
30   One moment I see the stillness of agony,
Something frozen in the silence that dare not be
Loosed, one moment the darkness frightens me.

Then among the averted pansies, beneath the high
White peaks of snow, at the foot of the sunken Christ
I stand in a chill of anguish, trying to say
The joy I bought was not too highly priced.

But he has gone, motionless, hating me,
Living as the mountains do, because they are strong,
With a pale, dead Christ on the crucifix of his heart,
40   And breathing the frozen memory of his wrong.

Still in his nostrils the frozen breath of despair,
And heart like a cross that bears dead agony
Of naked love, clenched in his fists the shame,
And in his belly the smouldering hate of me.

And I, as I stand in the cold, averted flowers,
Feel the shame-wounds in his hands pierce through my
        own,
And breathe despair that turns my lungs to stone
And know the dead Christ weighing on my bone.

Giorno Dei Morti

Along the avenue of cypresses,
All in their scarlet cloaks and surplices
Of linen, go the chanting choristers,
The priests in gold and black, the villagers...

And all along the path to the cemetery
The round dark heads of men crowd silently,
And black-scarved faces of womenfolk, wistfully
Watch at the banner of death, and the mystery.

And at the foot of a grave a father stands
10   With sunken head, and forgotten, folded hands;
And at the foot of a grave a mother kneels
With pale shut face, nor either hears nor feels

The coming of the chanting choristers
Between the avenue of cypresses,
The silence of the many villagers,
The candle-flames beside the surplices.

Song of a Man Who Has Come Through

Not I, not I, but the wind that blows through me!
A fine wind is blowing the new direction of Time.
If only I let it bear me, carry me, if only it carry me!
If only I am sensitive, subtle, oh, delicate, a winged gift!
If only, most lovely of all, I yield myself and am borrowed
By the fine, fine wind that takes its course through the
    chaos of the world
Like a fine, an exquisite chisel, a wedge-blade inserted;
If only I am keen and hard like the sheer tip of a wedge
Driven by invisible blows,
10   The rock will split, we shall come at the wonder, we
    shall find the Hesperides.

Oh, for the wonder that bubbles into my soul,
I would be a good fountain, a good well-head,
Would blur no whisper, spoil no expression.

What is the knocking?
What is the knocking at the door in the night?
It is somebody wants to do us harm.

No, no, it is the three strange angels.
Admit them, admit them.

Craving for Spring

I wish it were spring in the world.

Let it be spring!
Come, bubbling, surging tide of sap!

Come, rush of creation!
Come, life! surge through this mass of mortification!
Come, sweep away these exquisite, ghastly first-flowers,
    which are rather last-flowers!
Come, thaw down their cool portentousness, dissolve
    them:
snowdrops, straight, death-veined exhalation of white
    and purple crocuses,
flowers of the penumbra, issue of corruption, nourished
    in mortification,
10 jets of exquisite finality;
Come, spring, make havoc of them!

I trample on the snowdrops, it gives me pleasure to tread
    down the jonquils,
to destroy the chill Lent lilies;
for I am sick of them, their faint-bloodedness,
slow-blooded, icy-fleshed, portentous.

I want the fine, kindling wine-sap of spring,
gold, and of inconceivably fine, quintessential
    brightness,
rare almost as beams, yet overwhelmingly potent,
strong like the greatest force of world-balancing.

20 This is the same that picks up the harvest of wheat
and rocks it, tons of grain, on the ripening wind;
the same that dangles the globe-shaped pleiads of fruit
temptingly in mid-air, between a playful thumb and
    finger;

oh, and suddenly, from out of nowhere, whirls the pear-
        bloom,
upon us, and apple- and almond- and apricot- and
        quince-blossom,
storms and cumulus clouds of all imaginable blossom
about our bewildered faces,
though we do not worship.

I wish it were spring
30   cunningly blowing on the fallen sparks, odds and ends of
        the old, scattered fire,
and kindling shapely little conflagrations
curious long-legged foals, and wide-eared calves, and
        naked sparrow-bubs.

I wish that spring
would start the thundering traffic of feet
new feet on the earth, beating with impatience.

I wish it were spring, thundering
delicate, tender spring.
I wish these brittle, frost-lovely flowers of passionate,
        mysterious corruption
were not yet to come still more from the still-flickering
        discontent.

40   Oh, in the spring, the bluebell bows him down for very
        exuberance,
exulting with secret warm excess,
bowed down with his inner magnificence!

Oh, yes, the gush of spring is strong enough
to toss the globe of earth like a ball on a water-jet
dancing sportfully;
as you see a tiny celluloid ball tossing on a squirt of
        water
for men to shoot at, penny-a-time, in a booth at a fair.

The gush of spring is strong enough
to play with the globe of earth like a ball on a fountain;
50   At the same time it opens the tiny hands of the hazel
with such infinite patience.
The power of the rising, golden, all-creative sap could
    take the earth
and heave it off among the stars, into the invisible;
the same sets the throstle at sunset on a bough
singing against the blackbird;
comes out in the hesitating tremor of the primrose,
and betrays its candour in the round white strawberry
    flower,
is dignified in the foxglove, like a Red-Indian brave.

Ah come, come quickly, spring!
60   Come and lift us towards our culmination, we myriads;
we who have never flowered, like patient cactuses.
Come and lift us to our end, to blossom, bring us to our
    summer,
we who are winter-weary in the winter of the world.

Come making the chaffinch nests hollow and cosy,
come and soften the willow buds till they are puffed and
    furred,
then blow them over with gold.
Come and cajole the gawky colt's -foot flowers.

Come quickly, and vindicate us
against too much death.
70   Come quickly, and stir the rotten globe of the world
    from within,
burst it with germination, with world anew.
Come now, to us, your adherents, who cannot flower
    from the ice.

All the world gleams with the lilies of Death the
    Unconquerable,
but come, give us our turn.
Enough of the virgins and lilies, of passionate,
    suffocating perfume of corruption,
no more narcissus perfume, lily harlots, the blades of
    sensation
piercing the flesh to blossom of death.
Have done, have done with this shuddering, delicious
    business
of thrilling ruin in the flesh, of pungent passion, of rare,
    death-edged ecstasy.

80   Give us our turn, give us a chance, let our hour strike,
O soon, soon!
Let the darkness turn violet with rich dawn.
Let the darkness be warmed, warmed through to a ruddy
    violet,
incipient purpling towards summer in the world of the
    heart of man.

Are the violets already here!
Show me! I tremble so much to hear it, that even now
on the threshold of spring, I fear I shall die.
Show me the violets that are out.

Oh, if it be true, and the living darkness of the blood of
    man is purpling with violets
90   if the violets are coming out from under the rack of
    men, winter-rotten and fallen,
we shall have spring.
Pray not to die on this Pisgah blossoming with violets.
Pray to live through.

If you catch a whiff of violets from the darkness of the
    shadow of man
it will be spring in the world,
it will be spring in the world of the living;
wonderment organizing itself, heralding itself with the
    violets,
stirring of new seasons.

Ah, do not let me die on the brink of such anticipation!
100 Worse, let me not deceive myself.

                                  Zennor

from *Birds, Beasts and Flowers*

Peach

Would you like to throw a stone at me?
Here, take all that's left of my peach.

Blood-red, deep;
Heaven knows how it came to pass.
Somebody's pound of flesh rendered up.

Wrinkled with secrets
And hard with the intention to keep them.

Why, from silvery peach-bloom,
From that shallow-silvery wine-glass on a short stem
10   This rolling, dropping, heavy globule?

I am thinking of course of the peach, before I ate it.

Why so velvety, why so voluptuous heavy?
Why hanging with such inordinate weight?
Why so indented?

Why the groove?
Why the lovely, bivalve roundnesses?
Why the ripple down the sphere?
Why the suggestion of incision?

Why was not my peach round and finished like a billiard ball?
20   It would have been if man had made it.
Though I've eaten it now.

But it wasn't round and finished like a billiard ball.
And because I say so, you would like to throw something at
    me.

Here, you can have my peach stone.

San Gervasio

Medlars and Sorb-Apples

I love you, rotten,
Delicious rottenness.

I love to suck you out from your skins
So brown and soft and coming suave,
So morbid, as the Italians say.

What a rare, powerful, reminiscent flavour
Comes out of your falling through the stages of decay:
Stream within stream.

Something of the same flavour as Syracusan muscat wine
10 Or vulgar Marsala.

Though even the word Marsala will smack of preciosity
Soon in the pussyfoot West.

What is it?
What is it, in the grape turning raisin,
In the medlar, in the sorb-apple,
Wineskins of brown morbidity,
Autumnal excrementa;
What is it that reminds us of white gods?

Gods nude as blanched nut-kernels,
20 Strangely, half-sinisterly flesh-fragrant
As if with sweat,
And drenched with mystery.

Sorb-apples, medlars with dead crowns.
I say, wonderful are the hellish experiences,
Orphic, delicate
Dionysos of the Underworld.

A kiss, and a spasm of farewell, a moment's orgasm of
    rupture,
Then along the damp road alone, till the next turning.

And there, a new partner, a new parting, a new unfusing
    into twain,
30   A new gasp of further isolation,
A new intoxication of loneliness, among decaying, frost-
    cold leaves.

Going down the strange lanes of hell, more and more
    intensely alone,
The fibres of the heart parting one after the other
And yet the soul continuing, naked-footed, ever more
    vividly embodied
Like a flame blown whiter and whiter
In a deeper and deeper darkness
Ever more exquisite, distilled in separation.

So, in the strange retorts of medlars and sorb-apples
The distilled essence of hell.
40   The exquisite odour of leave-taking.
       Jamque vale!
Orpheus, and the winding, leaf-clogged, silent lanes of hell.

Each soul departing with its own isolation,
Strangest of all strange companions,
And best.

Medlars, sorb-apples,
More than sweet
Flux of autumn
Sucked out of your empty bladders

50   And sipped down, perhaps, with a sip of Marsala
So that the rambling, sky-dropped grape can add its
    savour to yours,
Orphic farewell, and farewell, and farewell
And the *ego sum* of Dionysos
The *sono io* of perfect drunkenness
Intoxication of final loneliness.

                San Gervasio

Almond Blossom

Even iron can put forth,
Even iron.

This is the iron age,
But let us take heart
Seeing iron break and bud,
Seeing rusty iron puff with clouds of blossom.

The almond-tree,
December's bare iron hooks sticking out of earth.

The almond-tree,
10 That knows the deadliest poison, like a snake
In supreme bitterness.

Upon the iron, and upon the steel,
Odd flakes as if of snow, odd bits of snow,
Odd crumbs of melting snow.

But you mistake, it is not from the sky;
From out the iron, and from out the steel,
Flying not down from heaven, but storming up,
Strange storming up from the dense under-earth
Along the iron, to the living steel
20 In rose-hot tips, and flakes of rose-pale snow
Setting supreme annunciation to the world.

Nay, what a heart of delicate super-faith,
Iron-breaking.
The rusty swords of almond-trees.

Trees suffer, like races, down the long ages.
They wander and are exiled, they live in exile through
        long ages
Like drawn blades never sheathed, hacked and gone black,

The alien trees in alien lands: and yet
The heart of blossom,
30 The unquenchable heart of blossom!

Look at the many-cicatrized frail vine, none more
    scarred and frail,
Yet see him fling himself abroad in fresh abandon
From the small wound-stump.

Even the wilful, obstinate, gummy fig-tree
Can be kept down, but he'll burst like a polyp into prolixity.

And the almond-tree, in exile, in the iron age!

This is the ancient southern earth whence the vases
    were baked, amphoras, craters, cantharus, œnochœ,
    and open-hearted cylix,
Bristling now with the iron of almond-trees

Iron, but unforgotten.
40 Iron, dawn-hearted,
Ever-beating dawn-heart, enveloped in iron against the
    exile, against the ages.

See it come forth in blossom
From the snow-remembering heart
In long-nighted January,
In the long dark nights of the evening star, and Sirius,
    and the Etna snow-wind through the long night.

Sweating his drops of blood through the long-nighted
    Gethsemane
Into blossom, into pride, into honey-triumph, into most
    exquisite splendour.
Oh, give me the tree of life in blossom
And the Cross sprouting its superb and fearless flowers!

50 Something must be reassuring to the almond, in the
        evening star, and the snow-wind, and the long, long
        night
    Some memory of far, sun-gentler lands,
    So that the faith in his heart smiles again
    And his blood ripples with that untellable delight of
        once-more-vindicated faith,
    And the Gethsemane blood at the iron pores unfolds,
        unfolds,
    Pearls itself into tenderness of bud
    And in a great and sacred forthcoming steps forth, steps
        out in one stride
    A naked tree of blossom, like a bridegroom bathing in
        dew, divested of cover,
    Frail-naked, utterly uncovered
    To the green night-baying of the dog-star, Etna's snow-
        edged wind
60 And January's loud-seeming sun.

    Think of it, from the iron fastness
    Suddenly to dare to come out naked, in perfection of
        blossom, beyond the sword-rust.
    Think, to stand there in full-unfolded nudity, smiling,
    With all the snow-wind, and the sun-glare, and the dog-
        star baying epithalamion.

    Oh, honey-bodied beautiful one
    Come forth from iron,
    Red your heart is.
    Fragile-tender, fragile-tender life-body,
    More fearless than iron all the time,
70 And so much prouder, so disdainful of reluctances.

In the distance like hoar-frost, like silvery ghosts
    communing on a green hill,
Hoar-frost-like and mysterious.
In the garden raying out
With a body like spray, dawn-tender, and looking about
With such insuperable, subtly-smiling assurance,
Sword-blade-born.

Unpromised,
No bounds being set.
Flaked out and come unpromised,
80 The tree being life-divine,
Fearing nothing, life-blissful at the core
Within iron and earth.

Knots of pink, fish-silvery
In heaven, in blue, blue heaven,
Soundless, bliss-full, wide-rayed, honey-bodied,
Red at the core,
Red at the core,
Knotted in heaven upon the fine light.

Open,
90 Open,
Five times wide open,
Six times wide open,
And given, and perfect;
And red at the core with the last sore-heartedness,
Sore-hearted-looking.

Fontana Vecchia

The Mosquito

When did you start your tricks,
Monsieur?

What do you stand on such high legs for?
Why this length of shredded shank,
You exaltation?

Is it so that you shall lift your centre of gravity upwards
And weigh no more than air as you alight upon me,
Stand upon me weightless, you phantom?

I heard a woman call you the Winged Victory
10 In sluggish Venice.
You turn your head towards your tail, and smile.

How can you put so much devilry
Into that translucent phantom shred
Of a frail corpus?

Queer, with your thin wings and your streaming legs,
How you sail like a heron, or a dull clot of air,
A nothingness.

Yet what an aura surrounds you;
Your evil little aura, prowling, and casting a numbness
    on my mind.

20 That is your trick, your bit of filthy magic:
Invisibility, and the anæsthetic power
To deaden my attention in your direction.

But I know your game now, streaky sorcerer.
Queer, how you stalk and prowl the air
In circles and evasions, enveloping me,
Ghoul on wings
Winged Victory.

Settle, and stand on long thin shanks
Eyeing me sideways, and cunningly conscious that I am
    aware,
30 You speck.

I hate the way you lurch off sideways into air
Having read my thoughts against you.

Come then, let us play at unawares,
And see who wins in this sly game of bluff.
Man or mosquito.

You don't know that I exist, and I don't know that you
    exist.
Now then!

It is your trump,
It is your hateful little trump,
40 You pointed fiend,
Which shakes my sudden blood to hatred of you:
It is your small, high, hateful bugle in my ear.

Why do you do it?
Surely it is bad policy.

They say you can't help it.

If that is so, then I believe a little in Providence
    protecting the innocent.
But it sounds so amazingly like a slogan,
A yell of triumph as you snatch my scalp.

Blood, red blood
50 Super-magical
Forbidden liquor.

I behold you stand
For a second enspasmed in oblivion,
Obscenely ecstasied

4

Sucking live blood,
My blood.

Such silence, such suspended transport,
Such gorging,
Such obscenity of trespass.

60   You stagger
As well as you may.
Only your accursed hairy frailty,
Your own imponderable weightlessness
Saves you, wafts you away on the very draught my anger
    makes in its snatching.

Away with a pæan of derision,
You winged blood-drop.

Can I not overtake you?
Are you one too many for me,
Winged Victory?
70   Am I not mosquito enough to out-mosquito you?

Queer, what a big stain my sucked blood makes
Beside the infinitesimal faint smear of you!
Queer, what a dim dark smudge you have disappeared
    into!

Siracusa

Fish

Fish, oh Fish,
So little matters!

Whether the waters rise and cover the earth
Or whether the waters wilt in the hollow places,
All one to you.

Aqueous, subaqueous,
Submerged
And wave-thrilled.

As the waters roll
10 Roll you.
The waters wash,
You wash in oneness
And never emerge.

Never know,
Never grasp.

Your life a sluice of sensation along your sides,
A flush at the flails of your fins, down the whorl of
    your tail,
And water wetly on fire in the grates of your gills;
Fixed water-eyes.

20 Even snakes lie together.

But oh, fish, that rock in water,
You lie only with the waters;
One touch.
No fingers, no hands and feet, no lips;
No tender muzzles,
No wistful bellies,
No loins of desire,
None.

You and the naked element,
30 Sway-wave.
Curvetting bits of tin in the evening light.

Who is it ejects his sperm to the naked flood?
In the wave-mother?
Who swims enwombed?
Who lies with the waters of his silent passion, womb-
    element?
—Fish in the waters under the earth.

What price *his* bread upon the waters?

Himself all silvery himself
In the element,
40 No more

Nothing more.

Himself,
And the element.
Food, of course!
Water-eager eyes,
Mouth-gate open
And strong spine urging, driving;
And desirous belly gulping.

Fear also!
50 He knows fear!
Water-eyes craning,
A rush that almost screams,
Almost fish-voice
As the pike comes....
Then gay fear, that turns the tail sprightly, from a
    shadow.

Food, and fear, and joie de vivre,
Without love.

The other way about:
Joie de vivre, and fear, and food,
60 All without love.

Quelle joie de vivre
Dans l'eau!
Slowly to gape through the waters,
Alone with the element;
To sink, and rise, and go to sleep with the waters;
To speak endless inaudible wavelets into the wave;
To breathe from the flood at the gills,
Fish-blood slowly running next to the flood, extracting
    fish-fire;
To have the element under one, like a lover;
70 And to spring away with a curvetting click in the air,
Provocative.
Dropping back with a slap on the face of the flood.
And merging oneself!

To be a fish!

So utterly without misgiving
To be a fish
In the waters.

Loveless, and so lively!
Born before God was love,
80 Or life knew loving.
Beautifully beforehand with it all.

Admitted, they swarm in companies,
Fishes.
They drive in shoals.
But soundless, and out of contact.

They exchange no word, no spasm, not even anger.
Not one touch.
Many suspended together, forever apart,
Each one alone with the waters, upon one wave with
    the rest.

90   A magnetism in the water between them only.

I saw a water-serpent swim across the Anapo.
And I said to my heart, *look, look at him!*
With his head up, steering like a bird!
He's a rare one, but he belongs...

But sitting in a boat on the Zeller lake
And watching the fishes in the breathing waters
Lift and swim and go their way—

I said to my heart, *who are these?*
And my heart couldn't own them...

100 A slim young pike, with smart fins
And grey-striped suit, a young cub of a pike
Slouching along away below, half out of sight,
Like a lout on an obscure pavement....

Aha, there's somebody in the know!

But watching closer
That motionless deadly motion,
That unnatural barrel body, that long ghoul nose...
I left off hailing him.

I had made a mistake, I didn't know him,
110 This grey, monotonous soul in the water,
This intense individual in shadow,
Fish-alive.

I didn't know his God,
I didn't know his God.

Which is perhaps the last admission that life has to
    wring out of us.

I saw, dimly,
Once a big pike rush,
And small fish fly like splinters.
And I said to my heart, *there are limits*
120 *To you, my heart;*
And to the one God.
Fish are beyond me.

Other Gods
Beyond my range... gods beyond my God....

They are beyond me, are fishes.
I stand at the pale of my being
And look beyond, and see
Fish, in the outerwards,
As one stands on a bank and looks in.

130 I have waited with a long rod
And suddenly pulled a gold-and-greenish, lucent fish
    from below,
And had him fly like a halo round my head,
Lunging in the air on the line.

Unhooked his gorping, water-horny mouth,
And seen his horror-tilted eye,
His red-gold, water-precious, mirror-flat bright eye;
And felt him beat in my hand, with mucous, leaping
    life-throb.
And my heart accused itself
Thinking: *I am not the measure of creation.*
140 *This is beyond me, this fish.*
His God stands outside my God.

And the gold-and-green pure lacquer-mucus comes off
    in my hand,

And the red-gold mirror-eye stares and dies,
And the water-suave contour dims.

But not before I have had to know
He was born in front of my sunrise,
Before my day.

He outstarts me.
And I, a many-fingered horror of daylight to him,
150 Have made him die.

Fishes
With their gold, red eyes, and green-pure gleam, and
    under-gold,
And their pre-world loneliness,
And more-than-lovelessness,
And white meat;
They move in other circles.

Outsiders.
Water-wayfarers.
Things of one element.
160 Aqueous,
Each by itself.

Cats, and the Neapolitans,
Sulphur sun-beasts,
Thirst for fish as for more-than-water;
Water-alive
To quench their over-sulphureous lusts.

But I, I only wonder
And don't know.
I don't know fishes.

170 In the beginning
Jesus was called The Fish...
And in the end.

Zell-am-See

Man and Bat

When I went into my room, at mid-morning,
Say ten o'clock...
My room, a crash-box over that great stone rattle
The Via de' Bardi....

When I went into my room at mid-morning,
Why?... a bird!

A bird
Flying round the room in insane circles.

In insane circles!
10   *... A bat!*

A disgusting bat
At mid-morning!...

Out! Go out!

Round and round and round
With a twitchy, nervous, intolerable flight,
And a neurasthenic lunge,
And an impure frenzy;
A bat, big as a swallow.

Out, out of my room!

20   The venetian shutters I push wide
To the free, calm upper air;
Loop back the curtains....

Now out, out from my room!

So to drive him out, flicking with my white
        handkerchief: *Go!*
But he will not.

Round and round and round
In an impure haste,
Fumbling, a beast in air,
And stumbling, lunging and touching the walls, the
    bell-wires
30   About my room!

Always refusing to go out into the air
Above that crash-gulf of the Via de' Bardi,
Yet blind with frenzy, with cluttered fear.

At last he swerved into the window bay,
But blew back, as if an incoming wind blew him in
    again.
A strong inrushing wind.

And round and round and round!
Blundering more insane, and leaping, in throbs, to
    clutch at a corner,
At a wire, at a bell-rope:
40   On and on, watched relentless by me, round and round
    in my room,
Round and round and dithering with tiredness and haste
    and increasing delirium
Flicker-splashing round my room.

I would not let him rest;
Not one instant cleave, cling like a blot with his breast
    to the wall
In an obscure corner.
Not an instant!

I flicked him on,
Trying to drive him through the window.
Again he swerved into the window bay
50   And I ran forward, to frighten him forth.

But he rose, and from a terror worse than me he flew
    past me
Back into my room, and round, round, round in my room
Clutch, cleave, stagger,
Dropping about the air
Getting tired.

Something seemed to blow him back from the window
Every time he swerved at it;
Back on a strange parabola, then round, round, dizzy in
    my room.

He *could* not go out,
60   I also realized...
It was the light of day which he could not enter,
Any more than I could enter the white-hot door of a
    blast furnace.

He could not plunge into the daylight that streamed at
    the window.
It was asking too much of his nature.

Worse even than the hideous terror of me with my
    handkerchief
Saying: *Out, go out!...*
Was the horror of white daylight in the window!

So I switched on the electric light, thinking: *Now
The outside will seem brown...*

70   But no.
The outside did not seem brown.
And he did not mind the yellow electric light.

Silent!
He was having a silent rest.
But never!
Not in my room.

Round and round and round
Near the ceiling as if in a web,
Staggering;
80   Plunging, falling out of the web,
Broken in heaviness,
Lunging blindly,
Heavier;
And clutching, clutching for one second's pause,
Always, as if for one drop of rest,
One little drop.

And I!
Never, I say....
Get out!

90   Flying slower,
Seeming to stumble, to fall in air.
Blind-weary.

Yet never able to pass the whiteness of light into
        freedom...
A bird would have dashed through, come what might.

Fall, sink, lurch, and round and round
Flicker, flicker-heavy;
Even wings heavy;
And cleave in a high corner for a second, like a clot,
        also a prayer.

But no.
100   *Out, you beast.*

Till he fell in a corner, palpitating, spent.
And there, a clot, he squatted and looked at me.
With sticking-out, bead-berry eyes, black,
And improper derisive ears,
And shut wings,
And brown, furry body.

Brown, nut-brown, fine fur!
But it might as well have been hair on a spider; thing
With long, black-paper ears.

110 So, a dilemma!
He squatted there like something unclean.

No, he must not squat, nor hang, obscene, in my room!

Yet nothing on earth will give him courage to pass the
sweet fire of day.

What then?
Hit him and kill him and throw him away?

Nay,
I didn't create him.
Let the God that created him be responsible for his
death...
Only, in the bright day, I will not have this clot in my
room.

120 Let the God who is maker of bats watch with them in
their unclean corners....
I admit a God in every crevice,
But not bats in my room;
Nor the God of bats, while the sun shines.

So out, out, you brute!...
And he lunged, flight-heavy, away from me, sideways,
a sghembo!
And round and round and round my room, a clot with
wings,
Impure even in weariness.

Wings dark skinny and flapping the air,
Lost their flicker.
130 Spent.

He fell again with a little thud
Near the curtain on the floor.
And there lay.

Only life has a way out.
And the human soul is fated to wide-eyed responsibility
In life.

So I picked him up in a flannel jacket,
Well covered, lest he should bite me.
For I would have had to kill him if he'd bitten me, the
    impure one....
140   And he hardly stirred in my hand, muffled up.

Hastily, I shook him out of the window.

And away he went!
Fear craven in his tail.
Great haste, and straight, almost bird straight above the
    Via de' Bardi.
Above that crash-gulf of exploding whips,
Towards the Borgo San Jacopo.

And now, at evening, as he flickers over the river
Dipping with petty triumphant flight, and tittering over
    the sun's departure,
I believe he chirps, pipistrello, seeing me here on this
    terrace writing:
150   *There he sits, the long loud one!*
But I am greater than he...
I escaped him....

Florence

Snake

A snake came to my water-trough
On a hot, hot day, and I in pyjamas for the heat,
To drink there.

In the deep, strange-scented shade of the great dark
    carob-tree
I came down the steps with my pitcher
And must wait, must stand and wait, for there he was at
    the trough before me.

He reached down from a fissure in the earth-wall in the
    gloom
And trailed his yellow-brown slackness soft-bellied
    down, over the edge of the stone trough
And rested his throat upon the stone bottom,
10 And where the water had dripped from the tap, in a
    small clearness,
He sipped with his straight mouth,
Softly drank through his straight gums, into his slack
    long body,
Silently.

Someone was before me at my water-trough,
And I, like a second comer, waiting.

He lifted his head from his drinking, as cattle do,
And looked at me vaguely, as drinking cattle do,
And flickered his two-forked tongue from his lips, and
    mused a moment,
And stooped and drank a little more,
20 Being earth-brown, earth-golden from the burning
    bowels of the earth
On the day of Sicilian July, with Etna smoking.

The voice of my education said to me
He must be killed,
For in Sicily the black, black snakes are innocent, the
    gold are venomous.

And voices in me said, If you were a man
You would take a stick and break him now, and finish
    him off.

But must I confess how I liked him,
How glad I was he had come like a guest in quiet, to
    drink at my water-trough
And depart peaceful, pacified, and thankless,
30   Into the burning bowels of this earth?

Was it cowardice, that I dared not kill him?
Was it perversity, that I longed to talk to him?
Was it humility, to feel so honoured?
I felt so honoured.

And yet those voices:
If you were not afraid, you would kill him!

And truly I was afraid, I was most afraid,
But even so, honoured still more
That he should seek my hospitality
40   From out the dark door of the secret earth.

He drank enough
And lifted his head, dreamily, as one who has drunken,
And flickered his tongue like a forked night on the air,
    so black,
Seeming to lick his lips,
And looked around like a god, unseeing, into the air,
And slowly turned his head,
And slowly, very slowly, as if thrice adream,

Proceeded to draw his slow length curving round
And climb again the broken bank of my wall-face.

50 And as he put his head into that dreadful hole,
And as he slowly drew up, snake-easing his shoulders,
    and entered farther,
A sort of horror, a sort of protest against his withdrawing
    into that horrid black hole,
Deliberately going into the blackness, and slowly
    drawing himself after,
Overcame me now his back was turned.

I looked round, I put down my pitcher.
I picked up a clumsy log
And threw it at the water-trough with a clatter.

I think it did not hit him,
But suddenly that part of him that was left behind
    convulsed in undignified haste,
60 Writhed like lightning, and was gone
Into the black hole, the earth-lipped fissure in the wall-
    front,
At which, in the intense still noon, I stared with
    fascination.

And immediately I regretted it.
I thought how paltry, how vulgar, what a mean act!
I despised myself and the voices of my accursed human
    education.

And I thought of the albatross,
And I wished he would come back, my snake.

For he seemed to me again like a king,
Like a king in exile, uncrowned in the underworld,
70 Now due to be crowned again.

And so, I missed my chance with one of the lords
Of life.
And I have something to expiate;
A pettiness.

Taormina

Baby Tortoise

You know what it is to be born alone,
Baby tortoise!

The first day to heave your feet little by little from the
    shell,
Not yet awake,
And remain lapsed on earth,
Not quite alive.

A tiny, fragile, half-animate bean.

To open your tiny break-mouth, that looks as if it would
    never open,
Like some iron door;
10   To lift the upper hawk-beak from the lower base
And reach your skinny little neck
And take your first bite at some dim bit of herbage,
Alone, small insect,
Tiny bright-eye,
Slow one.

To take your first solitary bite
And move on your slow, solitary hunt.
Your bright, dark little eye,
Your eye of a dark disturbed night,
20   Under its slow lid, tiny baby tortoise,
So indomitable.

No one ever heard you complain.

You draw your head forward, slowly, from your little
    wimple
And set forward, slow-dragging, on your four-pinned
    toes,
Rowing slowly forward.
Whither away, small bird?
Rather like a baby working its limbs,
Except that you make slow, ageless progress
And a baby makes none.

30   The touch of sun excites you,
And the long ages, and the lingering chill
Make you pause to yawn,
Opening your impervious mouth,
Suddenly beak-shaped, and very wide, like some
    suddenly gaping pincers;
Soft red tongue, and hard thin gums,
Then close the wedge of your little mountain front,
Your face, baby tortoise.

Do you wonder at the world, as slowly you turn your
    head in its wimple
And look with laconic, black eyes?
40   Or is sleep coming over you again,
The non-life?

You are so hard to wake.

Are you able to wonder?
Or is it just your indomitable will and pride of the first
    life
Looking round
And slowly pitching itself against the inertia
Which had seemed invincible?

The vast inanimate,
And the fine brilliance of your so tiny eye,
50   Challenger.

Nay, tiny shell-bird,
What a huge vast inanimate it is, that you must row
    against,
What an incalculable inertia.

Challenger,
Little Ulysses, fore-runner,
No bigger than my thumb-nail,
Buon viaggio.

All animate creation on your shoulder,
Set forth, little Titan, under your battle-shield.

60   The ponderous, preponderate,
Inanimate universe;
And you are slowly moving, pioneer, you alone.

How vivid your travelling seems now, in the troubled
    sun-shine,
Stoic, Ulyssean atom;
Suddenly hasty, reckless, on high toes.

Voiceless little bird,
Resting your head half out of your wimple
In the slow dignity of your eternal pause.
Alone, with no sense of being alone,
70   And hence six times more solitary;
Fulfilled of the slow passion of pitching through im-
    memorial ages
Your little round house in the midst of chaos.

Over the garden earth,
Small bird,
Over the edge of all things.

Traveller,
With your tail tucked a little on one side
Like a gentleman in a long-skirted coat.

All life carried on your shoulder,
80　Invincible fore-runner.

Tortoise Shout

I thought he was dumb,
I said he was dumb,
Yet I've heard him cry.

First faint scream,
Out of life's unfathomable dawn,
Far off, so far, like a madness, under the horizon's
　　dawning rim,
Far, far off, far scream.

Tortoise *in extremis*.

Why were we crucified into sex?
10　Why were we not left rounded off, and finished in
　　ourselves,
As we began,
As he certainly began, so perfectly alone?

A far, was-it-audible scream,
Or did it sound on the plasm direct?

Worse than the cry of the new-born,
A scream,
A yell,
A shout,
A pæan,
20　A death-agony,

A birth-cry,
A submission,
All tiny, tiny, far away, reptile under the first dawn.

War-cry, triumph, acute-delight, death-scream reptilian,
Why was the veil torn?
The silken shriek of the soul's torn membrane?
The male soul's membrane
Torn with a shriek half music, half horror.

Crucifixion.

30   Male tortoise, cleaving behind the hovel-wall of that
      dense female,
Mounted and tense, spread-eagle, out-reaching out of
      the shell
In tortoise-nakedness,
Long neck, and long vulnerable limbs extruded, spread-
      eagle over her house-roof,
And the deep, secret, all-penetrating tail curved
      beneath her walls,
Reaching and gripping tense, more reaching anguish in
      uttermost tension
Till suddenly, in the spasm of coition, tupping like a
      jerking leap, and oh!
Opening its clenched face from his outstretched neck
And giving that fragile yell, that scream,
Super-audible,

40   From his pink, cleft, old-man's mouth,
Giving up the ghost,
Or screaming in Pentecost, receiving the ghost.

His scream, and his moment's subsidence,
The moment of eternal silence,
Yet unreleased, and after the moment, the sudden,
      startling jerk of coition, and at once

The inexpressible faint yell—
And so on, till the last plasm of my body was melted
    back
To the primeval rudiments of life, and the secret.

So he tups, and screams
50 Time after time that frail, torn scream
After each jerk, the longish interval,
The tortoise eternity,
Age-long, reptilian persistence,
Heart-throb, slow hearth-throb, persistent for the next
    spasm.

I remember, when I was a boy,
I heard the scream of a frog, which was caught with his
    foot in the mouth of an up-starting snake;
I remember when I first heard bull-frogs break into
    sound in the spring;
I remember hearing a wild goose out of the throat of night
Cry loudly, beyond the lake of waters;
60 I remember the first time, out of a bush in the darkness,
    a nightingale's piercing cries and gurgles startled the
    depths of my soul;
I remember the scream of a rabbit as I went through a
    wood at midnight;
I remember the heifer in her heat, blorting and blorting
    through the hours, persistent and irrepressible;
I remember my first terror hearing the howl of weird,
    amorous cats;
I remember the scream of a terrified, injured horse, the
    sheet-lightning,
And running away from the sound of a woman in
    labour, something like an owl whooing,
And listening inwardly to the first bleat of a lamb,

The first wail of an infant,
And my mother singing to herself,
And the first tenor singing of the passionate throat of a
    young collier, who has long since drunk himself to
    death,
70 The first elements of foreign speech
On wild dark lips.

And more than all these,
And less than all these,
This last,
Strange, faint coition yell
Of the male tortoise at extremity,
Tiny from under the very edge of the farthest far-off
    horizon of life.

The Cross,
The wheel on which our silence first is broken,
80 Sex, which breaks up our integrity, our single
    inviolability, our deep silence,
Tearing a cry from us.

Sex, which breaks us into voice, sets us calling across
    the deeps, calling, calling for the complement,
Singing, and calling, and singing again, being answered,
    having found.

Torn, to become whole again, after long seeking for
    what is lost,
The same cry from the tortoise as from Christ, the
    Osiris-cry of abandonment,
That which is whole, torn asunder,
That which is in part, finding its whole again
    throughout the universe.

Turkey-Cock

You ruffled black blossom,
You glossy dark wind.

Your sort of gorgeousness,
Dark and lustrous
And skinny repulsive
And poppy-glossy,
Is the gorgeousness that evokes my most puzzled
    admiration.

Your aboriginality
Deep, unexplained,
10 Like a Red Indian darkly unfinished and aloof,
Seems like the black and glossy seeds of countless
    centuries.

Your wattles are the colour of steel-slag which has been
    red-hot
And is going cold,
Cooling to a powdery, pale-oxydized sky-blue.

Why do you have wattles, and a naked, wattled head?
Why do you arch your naked-set eye with a more-than-
    comprehensible arrogance?

The vulture is bald, so is the condor, obscenely,
But only you have thrown this amazing mantilla of
    oxydized sky-blue
And hot red over you.

20 This queer dross shawl of blue and vermilion,
Whereas the peacock has a diadem.

I wonder why.
Perhaps it is a sort of uncanny decoration, a veil of loose
    skin.

Perhaps it is your assertion, in all this ostentation, of raw
    contradictoriness.
Your wattles drip down like a shawl to your breast
And the point of your mantilla drops across your nose,
    unpleasantly.

Or perhaps it is something unfinished
A bit of slag still adhering, after your firing in the
    furnace of creation.

Or perhaps there is something in your wattles of a bull's
    dew-lap
30 Which slips down like a pendulum to balance the
    throbbing mass of a generous breast,
The over-drip of a great passion hanging in the balance.
Only yours would be a raw, unsmelted passion, that will
    not quite fuse from the dross.

You contract yourself,
You arch yourself as an archer's bow
Which quivers indrawn as you clench your spine
Until your veiled head almost touches backward
To the root-rising of your erected tail.
And one intense and backward-curving frisson
Seizes you as you clench yourself together
40 Like some fierce magnet bringing its poles together.

Burning, pale positive pole of your wattled head!
And from the darkness of that opposite one
The upstart of your round-barred, sun-round tail!

Whilst between the two, along the tense arch of your
    back
Blows the magnetic current in fierce blasts,
Ruffling black, shining feathers like lifted mail,
Shuddering storm wind, or a water rushing through.

Your brittle, super-sensual arrogance
Tosses the crape of red across your brow and down your
    breast
50 As you draw yourself upon yourself in insistence.

It is a declaration of such tension in will
As time has not dared to avouch, nor eternity been able
    to unbend
Do what it may.
A raw American will, that has never been tempered by
    life;
You brittle, will-tense bird with a foolish eye.

The peacock lifts his rods of bronze
And struts blue-brilliant out of the far East.
But watch a turkey prancing low on earth
Drumming his vaulted wings, as savages drum
60 Their rhythms on long-drawn, hollow, sinister drums.
The ponderous, sombre sound of the great drum of
    Huichilobos
In pyramid Mexico, during sacrifice.

Drum, and the turkey onrush
Sudden, demonic dauntlessness, full abreast,
All the bronze gloss of all his myriad petals
Each one apart and instant.
Delicate frail crescent of the gentle outline of white
At each feather-tip
So delicate:
70 Yet the bronze wind-bell suddenly clashing
And the eye overweening into madness.

Turkey-cock, turkey-cock,
Are you the bird of the next dawn?

Has the peacock had his day, does he call in vain,
    screecher, for the sun to rise?

The eagle, the dove, and the barnyard rooster, do they
    call in vain, trying to wake the morrow?
And do you await us, wattled father, Westward?
Will your yell do it?

Take up the trail of the vanished American
Where it disappeared at the foot of the crucifix.
80   Take up the primordial Indian obstinacy,
The more than human, dense insistence of will,
And disdain, and blankness, and onrush, and prise open
    the new day with them?

The East a dead letter, and Europe moribund…. Is that
    so?
And those sombre, dead, feather-lustrous Aztecs,
    Amerindians,
In all the sinister splendour of their red blood-sacrifices,
Do they stand under the dawn, half-godly, half-demon,
    awaiting the cry of the turkey-cock?

Or must you go through the fire once more, till you're
    smelted pure,
Slag-wattled turkey-cock,
Dross-jabot?

Fiesole

Humming-Bird

I can imagine, in some otherworld
Primeval-dumb, far back
In that most awful stillness, that only gasped and
    hummed,
Humming-birds raced down the avenues.

Before anything had a soul,
While life was a heave of Matter, half inanimate,

This little bit chipped off in brilliance
And went whizzing through the slow, vast, succulent
    stems.

I believe there were no flowers then,
10 In the world where the humming-bird flashed ahead of
    creation.
I believe he pierced the slow vegetable veins with his
    long beak.

Probably he was big
As mosses, and little lizards, they say, were once big.
Probably he was a jabbing, terrifying monster.

We look at him through the wrong end of the long
    telescope of Time,
Luckily for us.

Española

Kangaroo

In the northern hemisphere
Life seems to leap at the air, or skim under the wind
Like stags on rocky ground, or pawing horses, or springy
    scut-tailed rabbits.

Or else rush horizontal to charge at the sky's horizon,
Like bulls or bisons or wild pigs.

Or slip like water slippery towards its end,
As foxes, stoats, and wolves, and prairie dogs.

Only mice, and moles, and rats, and badgers, and
    beavers, and perhaps bears
Seem belly-plumbed to the earth's mid-navel.
10 Or frogs that when they leap come flop, and flop to the
    centre of the earth.

But the yellow antipodal Kangaroo, when she sits up,
Who can unseat her, like a liquid drop that is heavy, and
    just touches earth.

The downward drip
The down-urge.
So much denser than cold-blooded frogs.

Delicate mother Kangaroo
Sitting up there rabbit-wise, but huge, plumb-weighted,
And lifting her beautiful slender face, oh! so much more
    gently and finely lined than a rabbit's or than a hare's,
Lifting her face to nibble at a round white peppermint
    drop, which she loves, sensitive mother Kangaroo.

20 Her sensitive, long, pure-bred face.
Her full antipodal eyes, so dark,
So big and quiet and remote, having watched so many
    empty dawns in silent Australia.

Her little loose hands, and drooping Victorian shoulders.
And then her great weight below the waist, her vast pale
    belly
With a thin young yellow little paw hanging out, and
    straggle of a long thin ear, like ribbon,
Like a funny trimming to the middle of her belly, thin
    little dangle of an immature paw, and one thin ear.

Her belly, her big haunches
And, in addition, the great muscular python-stretch of
    her tail.

There, she shan't have any more peppermint drops.
30 So she wistfully, sensitively sniffs the air, and then turns,
    goes off in slow sad leaps

On the long flat skis of her legs,
Steered and propelled by that steel-strong snake of a tail.

Stops again, half turns, inquisitive to look back.
While something stirs quickly in her belly, and a lean
     little face comes out, as from a window,
Peaked and a bit dismayed,
Only to disappear again quickly away from the sight of
     the world, to snuggle down in the warmth,
Leaving the trail of a different paw hanging out.

Still she watches with eternal, cocked wistfulness!
How full her eyes are, like the full, fathomless, shining
     eyes of an Australian black-boy
40   Who has been lost so many centuries on the margins of
     existence!

She watches with insatiable wistfulness.
Untold centuries of watching for something to come,
For a new signal from life, in that silent lost land of the
     South.

Where nothing bites but insects and snakes and the sun,
     small life.
Where no bull roared, no cow ever lowed, no stag cried,
     no leopard screeched, no lion coughed, no dog
     barked,
But all was silent save for parrots occasionally, in the
     haunted blue bush.

Wistfully watching, with wonderful liquid eyes.
And all her weight, all her blood, dripping sack-wise
     down towards the earth's centre,
And the live little-one taking in its paw at the door of
     her belly.

50   Leap then, and come down on the line that draws to the
     earth's deep, heavy centre.

                                        Sydney

Mountain Lion

Climbing through the January snow, into the Lobo canyon
Dark grow the spruce-trees, blue is the balsam, water
    sounds still unfrozen, and the trail is still evident.

Men!
Two men!
Men! The only animal in the world to fear!

They hesitate.
We hesitate.
They have a gun.
We have no gun.

10   Then we all advance, to meet.

Two Mexicans, strangers, emerging out of the dark and
    snow and inwardness of the Lobo valley.
What are they doing here on this vanishing trail?

What is he carrying?
Something yellow.
A deer?

Qué tiene, amigo?
León—

He smiles, foolishly, as if he were caught doing wrong.
And we smile, foolishly, as if we didn't know.
20   He is quite gentle and dark-faced.

It is a mountain lion,
A long, long slim cat, yellow like a lioness.
Dead.

He trapped her this morning, he says, smiling foolishly.

Lift up her face,
Her round, bright face, bright as frost.

Her round, fine-fashioned head, with two dead ears;
And stripes in the brilliant frost of her face, sharp, fine
    dark rays,
Dark, keen, fine rays in the brilliant frost of her face.
30 Beautiful dead eyes.

Hermoso es!

They go out towards the open;
We go on into the gloom of Lobo.
And above the trees I found her lair,
A hole in the blood-orange brilliant rocks that stick up,
    a little cave.
And bones, and twigs, and a perilous ascent.

So, she will never leap up that way again, with the
    yellow flash of a mountain lion's long shoot!
And her bright striped frost-face will never watch any
    more, out of the shadow of the cave in the blood-
    orange rock,
Above the trees of the Lobo dark valley-mouth!

40 Instead, I look out.
And out to the dim of the desert, like a dream, never real;
To the snow of the Sangre de Cristo mountains, the ice
    of the mountains of Picoris,
And near across at the opposite steep of snow, green trees
    motionless standing in snow, like a Christmas toy.

And I think in this empty world there was room for me
    and a mountain lion.
And I think in the world beyond, how easily we might
    spare a million or two of humans
And never miss them.
Yet what a gap in the world, the missing white frost-face
    of that slim yellow mountain lion!

Lobo

from *Pansies*

How Beastly the Bourgeois Is

How beastly the bourgeois is
especially the male of the species—

Presentable, eminently presentable—
shall I make you a present of him?

Isn't he handsome? Isn't he healthy? Isn't he a fine
    specimen?
Doesn't he look the fresh clean Englishman, outside?
Isn't it God's own image? tramping his thirty miles a day
after partridges, or a little rubber ball?
wouldn't you like to be like that, well off, and quite the
    thing?

10 Oh, but wait!
Let him meet a new emotion, let him be faced with
    another man's need,
let him come home to a bit of moral difficulty, let life
    face him with a new demand on his understanding
and then watch him go soggy, like a wet meringue.
Watch him turn into a mess, either a fool or a bully.
Just watch the display of him, confronted with a new
    demand on his intelligence,
a new life-demand.

How beastly the bourgeois is
especially the male of the species—

Nicely groomed, like a mushroom
20 standing there so sleek and erect and eyeable—
and like a fungus, living on the remains of bygone life
sucking his life out of the dead leaves of greater life than
    his own.

And even so, he's stale, he's been there too long.
Touch him, and you'll find he's all gone inside
just like an old mushroom, all wormy inside, and hollow
under a smooth skin and an upright appearance.

Full of seething, wormy, hollow feelings
rather nasty—
How beastly the bourgeois is!

30 Standing in their thousands, these appearances, in damp
      England
what a pity they can't all be kicked over
like sickening toadstools, and left to melt back, swiftly
      into the soil of England.

When I Went to the Circus

When I went to the circus that had pitched on the
      waste lot
it was full of uneasy people
frightened of the bare earth and the temporary canvas
and the smell of horses and other beasts
instead of merely the smell of man.

Monkeys rode rather grey and wizened
on curly plump piebald ponies
and the children uttered a little cry—
and dogs jumped through hoops and turned somersaults
10 and then the geese scuttled in in a little flock
and round the ring they went to the sound of the whip
then doubled, and back, with a funny up-flutter of
      wings—
and the children suddenly shouted out.

Then came the hush again, like a hush of fear.

The tight-rope lady, pink and blonde and nude-looking,
    with a few gold spangles
footed cautiously out on the rope, turned prettily, spun
    round
bowed, and lifted her foot in her hand, smiled, swung
    her parasol
to another balance, tripped round, poised, and slowly sank
her handsome thighs down, down, till she slept her
    splendid body on the rope.

20 When she rose, tilting her parasol, and smiled at the
        cautious people
    they cheered, but nervously.

The trapeze man, slim and beautiful and like a fish in
    the air
swung great curves through the upper space, and came
    down like a star
—And the people applauded, with hollow, frightened
    applause.

The elephants, huge and grey, loomed their curved bulk
    through the dusk
and sat up, taking strange postures, showing the pink
    soles of their feet
and curling their precious live trunks like ammonites
and moving always with soft slow precision
as when a great ship moves to anchor.
30 The people watched and wondered, and seemed to
        resent the mystery that lies in beasts.

Horses, gay horses, swirling round and plaiting
in a long line, their heads laid over each other's necks;
they were happy, they enjoyed it;
all the creatures seemed to enjoy the game
in the circus, with their circus people.

But the audience, compelled to wonder
compelled to admire the bright rhythms of moving
    bodies
compelled to see the delicate skill of flickering human
    bodies
flesh flamey and a little heroic, even in a tumbling
    clown,
40 they were not really happy.
There was no gushing response, as there is at the film.

When modern people see the carnal body dauntless and
    flickering gay
playing among the elements neatly, beyond competition
and displaying no personality,
modern people are depressed.

Modern people feel themselves at a disadvantage.
They know they have no bodies that could play among
    the elements.
They have only their personalities, that are best seen
    flat, on the film,
flat personalities in two dimensions, imponderable and
    touchless.

50 And they grudge the circus people the swooping gay
    weight of limbs
that flower in mere movement,
and they grudge them the immediate, physical
    understanding they have with their circus beasts,
and they grudge them their circus-life altogether.

Yet the strange, almost frightened shout of delight that
    comes now and then from the children
shows that the children vaguely know how cheated they
    are of their birthright
in the bright wild circus flesh.

Whatever Man Makes

Whatever man makes and makes it live
lives because of the life put into it.
A yard of India muslin is alive with Hindu life.
And a Navajo woman, weaving her rug in the pattern of
    her dream
must run the pattern out in a little break at the end
so that her soul can come out, back to her.

But in the odd pattern, like snake-marks on the sand
it leaves its trail.

Good Husbands Make Unhappy Wives

Good husbands make unhappy wives
so do bad husbands, just as often;
but the unhappiness of a wife with a good husband
is much more devastating
than the unhappiness of a wife with a bad husband.

The Elephant is Slow to Mate

The elephant, the huge old beast,
        is slow to mate;
he finds a female, they show no haste
        they wait

for the sympathy in their vast shy hearts
        slowly, slowly to rouse
as they loiter along the river-beds
        and drink and browse

and dash in panic through the brake
10   of forest with the herd,
and sleep in massive silence, and wake
        together, without a word.

So slowly the great hot elephant hearts
        grow full of desire,
and the great beasts mate in secret at last,
        hiding their fire.

Oldest they are and the wisest of beasts
        so they know at last
how to wait for the loneliest of feasts
20   for the full repast.

They do not snatch, they do not tear;
        their massive blood
moves as the moon-tides, near, more near,
        till they touch in flood.

The Mess of Love

We've made a great mess of love
since we made an ideal of it.

The moment I swear to love a woman, a certain woman,
    all my life
that moment I begin to hate her.

The moment I even say to a woman: I love you!—
my love dies down considerably.

The moment love is an understood thing between us, we
    are sure of it,
it's a cold egg, it isn't love any more.

Love is like a flower, it must flower and fade;
10   if it doesn't fade, it is not a flower,
     it's either an artificial rag blossom, or an immortelle, for
        the cemetery.

The moment the mind interferes with love, or the will
    fixes on it,
or the personality assumes it as an attribute, or the ego
    takes possession of it,
it is not love any more, it's just a mess.
And we've made a great mess of love, mind-perverted,
    will-perverted, ego-perverted love.

Red-Herring

My father was a working man
    and a collier was he,
at six in the morning they turned him down
    and they turned him up for tea.

My mother was a superior soul
    a superior soul was she,
cut out to play a superior rôle
    in the god-damn bourgeoisie.

We children were the in-betweens
10   little non-descripts were we,
indoors we called each other *you*,
    outside, it was *tha* and *thee*.

But time has fled, our parents are dead
    we've risen in the world all three;
but still we are in-betweens, we tread
    between the devil and the deep cold sea.

O I am a member of the bourgeoisie
and a servant-maid brings me my tea—
But I'm always longing for someone to say:
20   'ark 'ere, lad! atween thee an' me

they're a' a b—d – lot o' ——s,
an' I reckon it's nowt but right
we should start an' kick their ——ses for 'em
an' tell 'em to ——.

Riches

When I wish I was rich, then I know I am ill.
Because, to tell the truth, I have enough as I am.
So when I catch myself thinking: Ah, if I was rich——!
I say to myself: Hello! I'm not well. My vitality is low.

To Women, as Far as I'm Concerned

The feelings I don't have I don't have.
The feelings I don' have, I won't say I have.
The feelings you say you have, you don't have.
The feelings you would like us both to have, we neither
   of us have.
The feelings people ought to have, they never have.
If people say they've got feelings, you may be pretty sure
   they haven't got them.

So if you want either of us to feel anything at all
you'd better abandon all idea of feelings altogether.

Desire is Dead

Desire may be dead
and still a man can be
a meeting place for sun and rain,
wonder outwaiting pain
as in a wintry tree.

Wages

The wages of work is cash.
The wages of cash is want more cash.
The wages of want more cash is vicious competition.
The wages of vicious competition is – the world we
    live in.

The work-cash-want circle is the viciousest circle
that ever turned men into fiends.

Earning a wage is a prison occupation
and a wage-earner is a sort of gaol-bird.
Earning a salary is a prison overseer's job,
10   a gaoler instead of a gaol-bird.

Living on your income is strolling grandly outside the
    prison
in terror lest you have to go in. And since the work-
    prison covers
almost every scrap of the living earth, you stroll up and
    down
on a narrow beat, about the same as a prisoner taking his
    exercise.

This is called universal freedom.

Relativity

I like relativity and quantum theories
because I don't understand them
and they make me feel as if space shifted
about like a swan that can't settle,
refusing to sit still and be measured;
and as if the atom were an impulsive thing
always changing its mind.

The Triumph of the Machine

They talk of the triumph of the machine,
but the machine will never triumph.

Out of the thousands and thousands of centuries of man
the unrolling of ferns, white tongues of the acanthus
     lapping at the sun,
for one sad century
machines have triumphed, rolled us hither and thither,
shaking the lark's nest till the eggs have broken.

Shaken the marshes, till the geese have gone
and the wild swans flown away singing the swan-song of
     us.

10 Hard, hard on the earth the machines are rolling,
but through some hearts they will never roll.

The lark nests in his heart
and the white swan swims in the marshes of his loins,
and through the wide prairies of his breast a young bull
     herds his cows,
lambs frisk among the daisies of his brain.

And at last
all these creatures that cannot die, driven back
into the uttermost corners of the soul,
will send up the wild cry of despair.

20   The trilling lark in a wild despair will trill down arrows
      from the sky,
    the swan will beat the waters in rage, white rage of an
      enraged swan,
    even the lambs will stretch forth their necks like serpents,
    like snakes of hate, against the man in the machine:
    even the shaking white poplar will dazzle like splinters
      of glass against him.

And against this inward revolt of the native creatures of
    the soul
mechanical man, in triumph seated upon the seat of his
    machine
will be powerless, for no engine can reach into the
    marshes and depths of a man.

So mechanical man in triumph seated upon the seat of
    his machine
will be driven mad from within himself, and sightless,
    and on that day
30   the machines will turn to run into one another
    traffic will tangle up in a long-drawn-out crash of
      collision
    and engines will rush at the solid houses, the edifice of
      our life
    will rock in the shock of the mad machine, and the
      house will come down.

Then, far beyond the ruin, in the far, in the ultimate,
    remote places
the swan will lift up again his flattened, smitten head

and look round, and rise, and on the great vaults of his
    wings
will sweep round and up to greet the sun with a silky
    glitter of a new day
and the lark will follow trilling, angerless again,
and the lambs will bite off the heads of the daisies for
    very friskiness.
40 But over the middle of the earth will be the smoky ruin
    of iron
the triumph of the machine.

For a Moment

For a moment, at evening, tired, as he stepped off the
    tram-car,
—the young tram-conductor in a blue uniform, to
    himself forgotten,——
and lifted his face up, with blue eyes looking at the
    electric rod which he was going to turn round,
for a moment, pure in the yellow evening light, he was
    Hyacinthus.

In the green garden darkened the shadow of coming rain
and a girl ran swiftly, laughing breathless, taking in her
    white washing
in rapid armfuls from the line, tossing it in the basket,
and so rapidly, and so flashing, fleeing before the rain
for a moment she was Io, Io, who fled from Zeus, or the
    Danaë.

10 When I was waiting and not thinking, sitting at a table
    on the hotel terrace
I saw suddenly coming towards me, lit up and uplifted
    with pleasure

advancing with the slow-swiftness of a ship backing her
    white sails into port
the woman who looks for me in the world
and for the moment she was Isis, gleaming, having
    found her Osiris.

For a moment, as he looked at me through his spectacles
pondering, yet eager, the broad and thick-set Italian
    who works in with me,
for a moment he was the Centaur, the wise yet horse-
    hoofed Centaur in whom I can trust.

Thought

Thought, I love thought.
But not the jiggling and twisting of already existent
    ideas
I despise that self-important game.
Thought is the welling up of unknown life into
    consciousness,
Thought is the testing of statements on the touchstone
    of the conscience,
Thought is gazing on to the face of life, and reading
    what can be read,
Thought is pondering over experience, and coming to a
    conclusion.
Thought is not a trick, or an exercise, or a set of dodges,
Thought is a man in his wholeness wholly attending.

from *Last Poems*

Middle of The World

This sea will never die, neither will it ever grow old
nor cease to be blue, nor in the dawn
cease to lift up its hills
and let the slim black ship of Dionysos come sailing in
with grape-vines up the mast, and dolphins leaping.

What do I care if the smoking ships
of the P. & O. and the Orient Line and all the other
    stinkers
cross like clock-work the Minoan distance!
They only cross, the distance never changes.

10   And now that the moon who gives men glistening
    bodies
is in her exaltation, and can look down on the sun
I see descending from the ships at dawn
slim naked men from Cnossos, smiling the archaic smile
of those that will without fail come back again,
and kindling little fires upon the shores
and crouching, and speaking the music of lost languages.

And the Minoan Gods, and the Gods of Tiryns
are heard softly laughing and chatting, as ever;
and Dionysos, young and a stranger
20   leans listening on the gate, in all respect.

Red Geranium and Godly Mignonette

Imagine that any mind ever *thought* a red geranium!
As if the redness of a red geranium could be anything
        but a sensual experience
and as if sensual experience could take place before
        there were any senses.
We know that even God could not imagine the redness
        of a red geranium
nor the smell of mignonette
when geraniums were not, and mignonette neither.
And even when they were, even God would have to
        have a nose
to smell at the mignonette.
You can't imagine the Holy Ghost sniffing at cherry-pie
        heliotrope.
10 Or the Most High, during the coal age, cudgelling his
        mighty brains
even if he had any brains: straining his mighty mind
to think, among the moss and mud of lizards and
        mastodons
to think out, in the abstract, when all was twilit green
        and muddy:
'Now there shall be tum-tiddly-um, and tum-tiddly-um,
hey-presto! scarlet geranium!'
We know it couldn't be done.

But imagine, among the mud and the mastodons
God sighing and yearning with tremendous creative
        yearning, in that dark green mess
oh, for some other beauty, some other beauty
20 that blossomed at last, red geranium, and mignonette.

The Man of Tyre

The man of Tyre went down to the sea
pondering, for he was Greek, that God is one and all
    alone and ever more shall be so.

And a woman who had been washing clothes in the
    pool of rock
where a stream came down to the gravel of the sea and
    sank in,
who had spread white washing on the gravel banked
    above the bay,
who had lain her shift on the shore, on the shingle slope,
who had waded to the pale green sea of evening, out to a
    shoal,
pouring sea-water over herself
now turned, and came slowly back, with her back to the
    evening sky.

10   Oh lovely, lovely with the dark hair piled up, as she
       went deeper, deeper down the channel, then rose
       shallower, shallower,
with the full thighs slowly lifting of the wader wading
    shorewards
and the shoulders pallid with light from the silent sky
    behind
both breasts dim and mysterious, with the glamorous
    kindness of twilight between them
and the dim blotch of black maidenhair like an indicator,
giving a message to the man—

So in the cane-brake he clasped his hands in delight
that could only be god-given, and murmured:
Lo! God is one god! But here in the twilight
godly and lovely comes Aphrodite out of the sea
20   towards me!

Whales Weep Not!

They say the sea is cold, but the sea contains
the hottest blood of all, and the wildest, the most
    urgent.

All the whales in the wider deeps, hot are they, as they
    urge
on and on, and dive beneath the icebergs.
The right whales, the sperm-whales, the hammer-heads,
    the killers
there they blow, there they blow, hot wild white breath
    out of the sea!

And they rock, and they rock, through the sensual
    ageless ages
on the depths of the seven seas,
and through the salt they reel with drunk delight
10   and in the tropics tremble they with love
and roll with massive, strong desire, like gods.
Then the great bull lies up against his bride
in the blue deep bed of the sea,
as mountain pressing on mountain, in the zest of life:
and out of the inward roaring of the inner red ocean of
    whale-blood
the long tip reaches strong, intense, like the maelstrom-
    tip, and comes to rest
in the clasp and the soft, wild clutch of a she-whale's
    fathomless body.

And over the bridge of the whale's strong phallus,
    linking the wonder of whales
the burning archangels under the sea keep passing, back
    and forth,
20   keep passing, archangels of bliss
from him to her, from her to him, great Cherubim

that wait on whales in mid-ocean suspended in the
    waves of the sea
great heaven of whales in the waters, old hierarchies.

And enormous mother whales lie dreaming suckling
    their whale-tender young
and dreaming with strange whale eyes wide open in the
    waters of the beginning and the end.

And bull-whales gather their women and whale-calves
    in a ring
when danger threatens, on the surface of the ceaseless
    flood
and range themselves like great fierce Seraphim facing
    the threat
encircling their huddled monsters of love.
30   And all this happens in the sea, in the salt
where God is also love, but without words:
and Aphrodite is the wife of whales
most happy, happy she!

and Venus among the fishes skips and is a she-dolphin
she is the gay, delighted porpoise sporting with love and
    the sea
she is the female tunny-fish, round and happy among
    the males
and dense with happy blood, dark rainbow bliss in the
    sea.

Invocation to the Moon

You beauty, O you beauty
you glistening garmentless beauty!
great lady, great glorious lady
greatest of ladies
crownless and jewelless and garmentless
because naked you are more wonderful than anything
    we can stroke—

Be good to me, lady, great lady of the nearest
heavenly mansion, and last!
Now I am at your gate, you beauty, you lady of all
    nakedness!
10   Now I must enter your mansion, and beg your gift
Moon, O Moon, great lady of the heavenly few.

Far and forgotten is the Villa of Venus the glowing
and behind me now in the gulfs of space lies the golden
    house of the sun,
and six have given me gifts, and kissed me god-speed
kisses of four great lords, beautiful, as they held me to
    their bosom in farewell
and kiss of the far-off lingering lady who looks over the
    distant fence of the twilight,
and one warm kind kiss of the lion with golden paws,

Now, lady of the Moon, now open the gate of your
    silvery house
and let me come past the silver bells of your flowers, and
    the cockleshells
20   into your house, garmentless lady of the last great gift:
who will give me back my lost limbs
and my lost white fearless breast
and set me again on moon-remembering feet
a healed, whole man, O Moon!

Lady, lady of the last house down the long, long street of
the stars
be good to me now, as I beg you, as you've always been
good to men
who begged of you and gave you homage
and watched for your glistening feet down the garden
path!

Bavarian Gentians

Not every man has gentians in his house
in soft September, at slow, sad Michaelmas.

Bavarian gentians, big and dark, only dark
darkening the day-time, torch-like with the smoking
blueness of Pluto's gloom,
ribbed and torch-like, with their blaze of darkness spread
blue
down flattening into points, flattened under the sweep of
white day
torch-flower of the blue-smoking darkness, Pluto's dark-
blue daze,
black lamps from the halls of Dis, burning dark blue,
giving off darkness, blue darkness, as Demeter's pale
lamps give off light,
10   lead me then, lead the way.

Reach me a gentian, give me a torch!
let me guide myself with the blue, forked torch of this
flower
down the darker and darker stairs, where blue is
darkened on blueness
even where Persephone goes, just now, from the frosted
September

to the sightless realm where darkness is awake upon the
    dark
and Persephone herself is but a voice
or a darkness invisible enfolded in the deeper dark
of the arms Plutonic, and pierced with the passion of
    dense gloom,
among the splendour of torches of darkness, shedding
    darkness on the lost bride and her groom.

In the Cities

In the cities
there is even no more any weather
the weather in town is always benzine, or else petrol
    fumes
lubricating oil, exhaust gas.

As over some dense marsh, the fumes
thicken, miasma, the fumes of the automobile
densely thicken in the cities.

In ancient Rome, down the thronged streets
no wheels might run, no insolent chariots.
10   Only the footsteps, footsteps
of people
and the gentle trotting of the litter-bearers.

In Minos, in Mycenae
in all the cities with lion gates
the dead threaded the air, lingering
lingering in the earth's shadow
and leaning towards the old hearth.

In London, New York, Paris
in the bursten cities

20   the dead tread heavily through the muddy air
      through the mire of fumes
      heavily, stepping weary on our hearts.

The Ship of Death

I

Now it is autumn and the falling fruit
and the long journey towards oblivion.

The apples falling like great drops of dew
to bruise themselves an exit from themselves.

And it is time to go, to bid farewell
to one's own self, and find an exit
from the fallen self.

II

Have you built your ship of death, O have you?
O build your ship of death, for you will need it.

10   The grim frost is at hand, when the apples will fall
      thick, almost thunderous, on the hardened earth.

And death is on the air like a smell of ashes!
Ah! can't you smell it?

And in the bruised body, the frightened soul
finds itself shrinking, wincing from the cold
that blows upon it through the orifices.

III

And can a man his own quietus make
with a bare bodkin?

With daggers, bodkins, bullets, man can make
20   a bruise or break of exit for his life;
      but is that a quietus, O tell me, is it quietus?

Surely not so! for how could murder, even self-murder
ever a quietus make?

IV

O let us talk of quiet that we know,
that we can know, the deep and lovely quiet
of a strong heart at peace!

How can we this, our own quietus, make?

V

Build then the ship of death, for you must take
the longest journey, to oblivion.

30   And die the death, the long and painful death
that lies between the old self and the new.

Already our bodies are fallen, bruised, badly bruised,
already our souls are oozing through the exit
of the cruel bruise.

Already the dark and endless ocean of the end
is washing in through the breaches of our wounds,
already the flood is upon us.

Oh build your ship of death, your little ark
and furnish it with food, with little cakes, and wine
40   for the dark flight down oblivion.

VI

Piecemeal the body dies, and the timid soul
has her footing washed away, as the dark flood rises.

We are dying, we are dying, we are all of us dying
and nothing will stay the death-flood rising within us
and soon it will rise on the world, on the outside world.

We are dying, we are dying, piecemeal our bodies are
     dying

and our strength leaves us,
and our soul cowers naked in the dark rain over the
    flood,
cowering in the last branches of the tree of our life.

VII

50 We are dying, we are dying, so all we can do
is now to be willing to die, and to build the ship
of death to carry the soul on the longest journey.

A little ship, with oars and food
and little dishes, and all accoutrements
fitting and ready for the departing soul.

Now launch the small ship, now as the body dies
and life departs, launch out, the fragile soul
in the fragile ship of courage, the ark of faith
with its store of food and little cooking pans
60 and change of clothes,
upon the flood's black waste
upon the waters of the end
upon the sea of death, where still we sail
darkly, for we cannot steer, and have no port.

There is no port, there is nowhere to go
only the deepening black darkening still
blacker upon the soundless, ungurgling flood
darkness at one with darkness, up and down
and sideways utterly dark, so there is no direction any
    more.
70 And the little ship is there; yet she is gone.
She is not seen, for there is nothing to see her by.
She is gone! gone! and yet
somewhere she is there.
Nowhere!

VIII

And everything is gone, the body is gone
completely under, gone, entirely gone.
The upper darkness is heavy on the lower,
between them the little ship
is gone
80 she is gone.

It is the end, it is oblivion.

IX

And yet out of eternity, a thread
separates itself on the blackness,
a horizontal thread
that fumes a little with pallor upon the dark.

Is it illusion? or does the pallor fume
A little higher?
Ah wait, wait, for there's the dawn,
the cruel dawn of coming back to life
90 out of oblivion.

Wait, wait, the little ship
drifting, beneath the deathly ashy grey
of a flood-dawn.

Wait, wait! even so, a flush of yellow
and strangely, O chilled wan soul, a flush of rose.

A flush of rose, and the whole thing starts again.

X

The flood subsides, and the body, like a worn sea-shell
emerges strange and lovely.
And the little ship wings home, faltering and lapsing
100 on the pink flood,
and the frail soul steps out, into her house again
filling the heart with peace.

Swings the heart renewed with peace
even of oblivion.

Oh build your ship of death, oh build it!
for you will need it.
For the voyage of oblivion awaits you.

Shadows

And if tonight my soul may find her peace
in sleep, and sink in good oblivion,
and in the morning wake like a new-opened flower
then I have been dipped again in God, and new-created.

And if, as weeks go round, in the dark of the moon
my spirit darkens and goes out, and soft, strange gloom
pervades my movements and my thoughts and words
then I shall know that I am walking still
with God, we are close together now the moon's in
    shadow.

10   And if, as autumn deepens and darkens
I feel the pain of falling leaves, and stems that break in
    storms
and trouble and dissolution and distress
and then the softness of deep shadows folding, folding
around my soul and spirit, around my lips
so sweet, like a swoon, or more like the drowse of a low,
    sad song
singing darker than the nightingale, on, on to the
    solstice
and the silence of short days, the silence of the year, the
    shadow,
then I shall know that my life is moving still
with the dark earth, and drenched

20   with the deep oblivion of earth's lapse and renewal.

And if, in the changing phases of man's life
I fall in sickness and in misery
my wrists seem broken and my heart seems dead
and strength is gone, and my life
is only the leavings of a life:

and still, among it all, snatches of lovely oblivion, and
     snatches of renewal
odd, wintry flowers upon the withered stem, yet new,
     strange flowers
such as my life has not brought forth before, new
     blossoms of me—

then I must know that still
30   I am in the hands [of] the unknown God,
he is breaking me down to his own oblivion
to send me forth on a new morning, a new man.

Notes

from *Early Poems*

Discord in Childhood

This is a surviving fragment from a sequence called *A Life History in Harmonies and Discords* most of which the young Lawrence destroyed along with other early poems. He later regretted the suppression of poems which *had the demon fuming in them* (Foreword to *Collected Poems*, 1928). The scene is one of a parental quarrel as overheard by a child. What associations are established between the human voices and the other sounds in the poem? What effect does the phrase *silence of blood* (8) have?

You could compare the poem with Lawrence's prose treatment of a similar experience in his novel, *Sons and Lovers* (Chapter 4).

Piano

The poem portrays the experience of being overwhelmed by nostalgia. The expression of such feelings in poetry can often seem over-indulgent. In deciding for yourself whether this poem *is* sentimental (and, if so, whether this is necessarily a criticism) much will depend on how precise and persuasive you find the diction, the chosen details, and the rhythm of the poem. For example, is *boom of the tingling strings* (3) aurally accurate or sloppily contradictory? Why might the mother's feet be *poised* (4), and how does the pause caused by the comma contribute to the meaning here? The poem has a regular rhyme scheme, but what is the effect of combining this with a movement that rarely pauses at the ends of lines? Are the references to the *old Sunday evenings at home* (7) and the *cosy parlour* (8) feebly indulgent or is the sentiment controlled by the poet's recognition of what is happening to him – *insidious mastery of song/Betrays me back* (5–6)? Does *glamour* (10) work in context or is it too obviously there for the rhyme? (See Tasks p. 172 for a chance to compare this with an earlier version of the poem.)

10 **appassionato** 'impassioned' (Italian). Used in musical notation to indicate the style of playing required.

The Wild Common

This poem is a fascinating, flawed tussle between the demon and the young man; forced rhymes and awkward rhythmic emphases cannot extinguish the frequent vitality of phrasing. The poem eroticizes the Narcissus myth in which a beautiful young man, indifferent to the love of others, becomes enamoured of his own reflection in water and pines away.

In Lawrence's version the young man enjoys a blissful return to nature. Self-love, far from being destructive, unifies male and female aspects of the divided self. Rather than standing unrequited upon the bank the poet achieves consummation by entering the water. In the figuring of the *deep pond* (13) as a woman, the ideas of a return to the mother's womb and an anticipation of future relationships may both be discerned (See Approaches pp. 139–140.) Chapter 4 of *Women in Love*, in which a man swimming in a lake is observed by two young women, provides opportunities for comparison.

Cherry Robbers

Explore how economically the poem evokes ideas of sex and cruelty, pleasure and wrongdoing. What implications arise from the juxtaposition of the dead birds and the prospective lovers? Are the tears to be drawn by accepting or declining the offer of love, or by a subsequent abandonment? The haunting quality of the poem perhaps arises from its air of anticipation: a sense of innocence amidst images of experience.

See *Sons and Lovers* Chapter 11 for a prose description of a similar incident.

7 **throstles** the song-thrush.
robberlings young or petty thieves.

Cruelty and Love

You may find the roles given to the man and woman in this poem disquieting. Do you think that the intensity with which Lawrence embraces the woman narrator's point of view is an indirect celebration and, in the final line an endorsement, of male dominance in love? How do the images accumulated in the poem further urge this idea upon the reader as 'natural'?

The poem may also be seen as an attempt by Lawrence to use a poetic fiction to resolve contradictory feelings he has about gender. Jessie Chambers, the girl-friend of Lawrence's youth, offers this recollection:

> He would tell me with vehemence that nature is red in tooth and claw, with the implication that 'nature' included human nature. Yet when he heard the cry of a rabbit tracked by a weasel he would shiver in pain.
>
> *D. H. Lawrence: A Personal Record*

Interestingly, in an earlier version of the poem, the snared rabbit was male. (See Approaches pp. 159–160.)

A Collier's Wife

This is the first in a cluster of poems in which Lawrence, normally hostile to received forms, works within the tradition of the dialect ballad.

This is originally an oral form of folk poetry in which a story is told, largely through dialogue, using speech drawn from a particular locality; Nottinghamshire dialect in this case. Lawrence is often accused of being unable to handle regular rhyme and rhythm so you might assess here the skill with which the formal versification combines with the rendering of freer speech patterns. A good poem of this sort will sustain the impression of naturalness of speech over an extended sequence of stanzas. Do the rhymes grate or seem trite, given the constraints imposed by the idioms of the wife?

You could also look at this poem as a study of a character in a state of shock: the to and fro of her complaints and practical concerns, her fussing and self-reassurance. Might not the wife's habitual scolding of her husband hint at a deeper bond of feeling, the more moving because it is not directly stated? (See Approaches (pp. 140–2) for more on the ballad form.) See *Sons and Lovers* Chapter 5 and the short story *Odour of Chrysanthemums* for accounts of similar incidents.

  7 **mard-'arsed** spoilt, soft.
 19 **scraightin'** crying, screaming.
 52 **club money** i.e. from miners' welfare club.

Violets

In this version of the poem the symbolic contrast between the white flowers (cold, formal, official) and the violets (warm, intimate, spontaneous), together with the differences of opinion between the sisters, are understated. A later revision appends a further stanza:

> But I thowt ter mysen, as that wor th'only bit
> O'warmth as 'e got down theer; th'rest wor stone cold.
> From that bit of a wench's bosom; 'e'd be glad of it,
> Gladder nor of thy lilies, if tha maun be told.

What is gained and what lost by this addition?

 25 **slive up** sneak up.
 29 **scraightin'** see note on line 19 of *A Collier's Wife* above.

End of Another Home-Holiday

On the page this poem presents a curious collection of various stanza forms, rhyme schemes, and free verse. (For an explanation of free verse see Approaches pp.136–8.) Reading it will reveal similar disturbances in the metre. Regular beats and emphases give way, at times, to rhythms which work against the apparent clarity of the stanza forms. How close a relationship is there between these discontinuities in the form and the emotions described in the poem? Is there a parallel between the son's troubled bid for independence and the poet's stylistic restlessness?

The subject of the poem is very close to Lawrence's personal experience. Do you find the expression of unresolved emotions in the poem embarrassingly overwrought? The son is torn between an assertion of the right to independence and a sense of guilt in claiming it; empathy and revulsion compete unstably in the presentation of the mother.

The search for a perspective on human emotional divisions through attention to non-human life forms is an interesting anticipation of Lawrence's work in *Birds, Beasts and Flowers*. See *Sons and Lovers* (Chapter 11) for a description of a closely-related incident where many of these symbols recur.

> 56 **corncrake** bird whose rasping, repetitive call is here associated with the mother's demands, or alternatively, with the voicing of a rival, if equally irksome, claim upon the son. Poignantly, the poem is quite unclear as to whether her behaviour is to be regarded as natural or unnatural.

After the Opera

Relaxed yet perfect as though its form precisely enacts the experience described, this is Lawrence's first, if passing, success in free verse. The exalted look of those privileged to watch an artistically shaped tragedy is contrasted with the exhausted look of chronic mundane sadness from the barman. The formerly confident poet artlessly admits to a sudden need for security.

The Bride

This and the poem which follows arise from the death of Lawrence's mother. In its images of a girl, a maiden, and then a bride, the poem reflects the transitions in a woman's life. The paradox that the body is old while the facial expression and posture are young gradually reveals that she has been restored to her youthful self in death, hopeful, perfect, as if arrested at the moment in life when her prospects for fulfilment were greatest. In its unashamed tenderness, it is a kind of love poem. This fact has led some readers to identify a possible *Oedipus Complex* in this poem – the desire of a son to supplant the father and possess the mother.

You may feel that the astonishing beauty of the last two lines provides a more rewarding focus of attention. *Sings* at the end of line 15 seems momentarily wishful until justified in *By its shape* in line 16. The exquisite quality of these lines, and the pain they issue from, may be gauged by comparison with this quotation from a recently discovered manuscript poem of Lawrence's called *Death-Pæan of a Mother*:

> But mouth, ah mouth half open
> Never to close again
> Never to speak again.
> Half open now as shouting
> In death!

The death of Lydia Lawrence is described, in fictionalized form as that of Mrs Morel, in Chapter 14 of *Sons and Lovers*.

Sorrow

The means by which this poem achieves its effect of casual precision may be partly explained by the unobtrusive rhyming of some lines across stanzas rather than within them, and also by the way the whole poem is organized as an explanation of its central image to an implied reader. In *Sons and Lovers* Paul Morel – the Lawrence figure – initially mistakes his mother's hairs on his coat for cigarette ash (Chapter 13).

Whether or Not

This is, in effect, a short story told through a poem cycle. It looks provocatively at the sex-before-marriage question. Do you see Lizzy Stainwright as decently chaste or sexually prim, forgiving or self-righteous? The poem seems poised between distaste for the domestication of the sex-impulse on the one hand, and its mis-direction on the other. Lawrence later turned against the ending in which he found *the voice of the commonplace me, not the demon*. In a revised version the otherwise taciturn Tim has the last word. Sexually unrepentant, he evades the grasp of both women:

> I'll say good-bye, Liz, to yer,
> Yer too much 'i' th'right for me.

An 'wi' 'er somehow it isn't right.
So good-bye, an' let's let be!

The moral dilemma posed in the title is not easily solved. In deciding which conclusion you find the more satisfying and/or plausible, it is worth noting that the earlier ending can hardly be described as 'happy'. See Approaches (pp. 141–2).

11 **crowflower**   crowfoot is a type of buttercup.
26 **otchel**   perhaps a misshapen person.
61 **pee-whips**   peewits, lapwings, birds whose name derives from their distinctive cry.
65 **smock-ravelled**   in a tangle, jumbled up.
66 **Larropin'**   stumbling.
114 **clawkin'**   clawing.
166 **colleyfoglin'**   manipulating.
167 **orts an' slarts**   left-overs.
173 **haffle an' caffle**   argue indecisively.
210 **ormin'**   despondent, despairing.
212 **scraight**   cry.

A Winter's Tale

This well-crafted, curiously conventional, poem responds well to analysis of its form. Do you find the rhyme scheme well handled? Are there any words obtrusively chosen for sound alone, *scarf* (5), perhaps? The scene is sharply visualized: the internal rhyme in line 11 gives the effect of plodding reluctance, *half Sobs* (7/8) uses rhythm and the line break to enact the sense, and the rhetorical questions give an effect of urgency. The tone carries an interesting tension between sympathy for the girl and puzzled irritation at her emotional persistence in the face of rejection.

Ballad of Another Ophelia

Lawrence wrote in a letter:

This poem – I am very proud of it – has got the quality of a troublesome dream that seems incoherent but is selected by another sort of consciousness. The latter part is the waking up part, yet never really awake, because she is mad.

Ophelia is a young woman in Shakespeare's play *Hamlet*. Spurned by Prince Hamlet after his initial advances to her, she goes mad. In fragmentary and highly suggestive speeches she reveals a surprising obsession with the sexual act. There is ambiguity as to whether she laments the loss of her virginity or its preservation.

A similar ambiguity accounts for the incoherence and mystery of the poem. Does the girl lament the loss of her lover or the cruelty of sex? Will the apples fail to ripen because they have been picked too early or because the sun (her lover) has withdrawn, leaving only rain? Male sexuality is figured in the yellow sun which ripens and the grey rat which destroys and at whose activities the sun seems to connive in the closing image. Sexual experience is desired and feared; related to fertility and to death. Is the implication that the girl has been driven mad by her inability to accept the contradictory nature of sexual experience?

How disturbing do you find the way sympathy with female suffering consorts with a mischievous celebration of man as lover and predator?

29 **garner:** storehouse, granary.

The Chief Mystery

This major early free verse poem shows Lawrence experimenting with rhythm, line length, layout, and syntactical repetition (see, for example, the uses of *then*, *and*, *whether*) to communicate a sense of religious ceremony in the loss and recovery of the self through sex. See Approaches (pp. 156–7) for a discussion of the relationship between religion and sex in Lawrence's poems.

from *Look! We Have Come Through!*

Bei Hennef

Lawrence felt this poem captured the beginning of a new phase of his emotional life. It was written at a railway station by a river in the Rhineland. He had left England and embarked on the relationship with Frieda Weekley (see Approaches p. 151). Fittingly, this poem also marks the beginning of an increasing commitment to free verse.

What risks do you feel Lawrence takes in this poem? The intimate second person address (*you...*), the avoidance of an explanation of the situation, the use of sound images rather than visual ones, the diction: simple to the point of banality, the shifts in tone and rhythm, the closeness to unmistakably personal emotion, the grandiose antitheses (lines 14–16) of the final movement, are all calculated technical risks. And yet the poem successfully communicates a sense of the insecurity of the lived moment. Look at the way the grammar of the poem (for example in line 20) and the emotional situation are left incomplete until closure is achieved in the discovery of the final line: the feeling of being complete can not be willed, nor can anxiety be banished by love.

A Young Wife

It is interesting that the pain of intense love and the heightened sense awareness that accompanies this should be given, apparently, from a woman's point of view here and that the man is shown as initiating her into perception of the primal darkness. The idea of a *dark sun* recurs in Lawrence's writing as an image of the life-source in which all opposites have their origin. You may see a connection here with *The torches of darkness* (19) in *Bavarian Gentians*. This passage from his novel *The Plumed Serpent* further defines the image:

> He looked up at the sun, and through the sun he saw the dark sun,
> the same that made the sun and the world and will swallow it
> again like a draught of water.

You may be surprised to discover how much rhyming the poem contains despite the free verse feel of the opening and concluding statements. What do you think the poem gains in tone, movement, and feeling from the alternation of two and four line stanzas? For a fictional treatment of the ebb and flow of fear, hostility, and tenderness in early married love, see *The Rainbow* Chapter 6. See also Approaches pp. 159–60.

Gloire de Dijon

The name of the rose which gives the poem its title is French for 'glory of Dijon' (a French city). Look up the word *glory* in a good dictionary and see how widely the poem draws upon its range of meaning. How well does the verbal sketching of the poem capture sound, movement, and the play of light? The significance of the rose image is clarified in the next poem. See Approaches p. 144 for further discussion of this poem.

Roses on the Breakfast Table

It has been felt that this is one of Lawrence's less successful poems because he *tries to channel it into a preconceived form* (Sandra Gilbert, *Acts of Attention*); equally it has been regarded as spontaneous, delicate and complete.

When read, does the poem come across as an uneasy attempt at regular metre or do you find its rhythms justified as *the natural lingering of the voice according to the feeling* (D. H. Lawrence)? Is the half-rhyme *cloth/loth* in the first stanza awkward? If so, does this lack of completion have an expressive role in the unfolding of the poem's meaning? Perhaps the sense of slight unease and resistance works well when set against the crisp rhyme of *roses/discloses* in which the poem encapsulates the new revelation: transience accepted as a condition of beauty in nature and in the self. Lawrence, as can also be seen in *Gloire de Dijon*, often uses the rose as a symbol for the state of perfect singleness in equilibrium achieved by happy lovers.

The poem is an intimate one, suggestive of an early phase in a sexual relationship. Is it fanciful to sense in the adjective *rumpled* (6) the suggestion of a bed as yet unmade? Does the poem objectify this situation or do you feel embarrassed as if intruding upon someone's privacy?

> 1 **roses we gathered** an echo of the first line of a poem by Robert Herrick, *Gather ye rosebuds while ye may* (*To the Virgins to make much of time*). Picking roses is a decorous image for accepting sexual opportunities.
> **Isar** a river in Bavaria, Southern Germany. Lawrence and Frieda stayed at Icking, on the Isar, shortly after their elopement.

Meeting Among the Mountains

See Approaches (p. 157) for a discussion of Lawrence's use of the idea of crucifixion in his poems. The pained eyes of the bullock wagon driver bring a guilty recognition to Lawrence of the suffering he has brought to Professor Ernest Weekley, Frieda's first husband, by taking up with his wife. How crucial is this biographical information to a satisfying reading of the poem?

  9 **Christ on the Cross** Lawrence wrote an essay, *Christs in the Tirol*, about the painted wooden sculptures of the crucifixion which are erected by the roadside in the Alps. Central to the poem is the idea that Lawrence's personal renewal has been achieved through another's anguish.

Giorno Dei Morti

The title is Italian for All Soul's Day or the Day of the Dead, in the Christian calendar an occasion for holding commemorative services. A companion poem, 'All Souls', addressed to his mother ends: *I am a naked candle burning on your grave.*

The measured pace of solemn ritual and the contrast between the poet who observes the scene and the bereaved who are caught up in it are most memorable. What do the repeated words and phrases contribute to the total effect?

  2 **surplices** white vestments worn over cassocks by clergy and choristers.

Song of a Man Who Has Come Through

Perhaps the title claims more than this cryptically allusive and mystically concluded poem can support. Central is the image of the wind which combines an artistic idea (inspiration), a Christian idea (the Holy Spirit, breath of God), and a pagan idea (cosmic life energy). In the opening line there are references to the exclamation of the German philosopher, Friedrich Nietzsche: *Not I! Not I but a God through my instrumentality*, and to the American poet, Walt Whitman, a major influence on Lawrence's free verse, whose *Song of Myself* is implicitly rebuked here. The poem articulates a Romantic view of the artist as the instrument of primal forces which speak through him. Lawrence hopes to be responsive to the new age he believes is beginning in the world as in his personal life. The mysterious arrival of the angels appears to provide assurance that his marriage is blessed.

10 **rock** perhaps the conscious self which must be split to allow the fountain of life to gush up from below.

Hesperides in Greek mythology, the Isles of the Blessed, a paradise where the golden apples grew.

17 **three strange angels** possibly the three nymphs, also called Hesperides, who guarded the apples; more probably, as in the Bible *Genesis 18*, the strangers who herald the birth of a son to Abraham and Sarah. Either way, the idea that the marriage will be fruitful is implicitly conveyed.

Craving for Spring

This gushing poem may best be understood as issuing from the state of sensibility invoked in the previous one. The assurance with which it celebrates the coming victory of the forces of life over the forces of death gains poignancy from the bathos or anti-climax of the final line. Lawrence hopes that the wintry age of destruction and death, which he believes the world is passing through, will end with the imminent conclusion of the First World War.

Free verse is dependent upon rhythmic momentum and a succession of fresh images. How successfully are these maintained?

22 **pleiads** clusters, as of stars.

73 **lilies of Death the Unconquerable** Lawrence often expressed a distaste for *beautiful dying decadent things with sad odours* as symbolized in the lilies here.

92 **Pisgah** a biblical mountain from which Moses saw the Promised Land.

from *Birds, Beasts and Flowers*

Peach

When read aloud, this tantalizing poem invites attention to the variety of its conversational tone, as Lawrence dangles the peach before us in language that evokes the qualities of the fruit he had just eaten. You may see the stone as the mystery at the centre of the peach which Lawrence cannot get at or you may feel it is simply the bit he does not want. Perhaps, given the sexual allure attributed to the peach and the fact that stoning is an ancient punishment for adultery, the offer of the stone may be read as a flaunting of the act of infidelity he had just committed with the fruit? If so, the second person mode of address, 'you', suggests that the poem can be read as a piece of teasing directed towards a wife or lover.

Medlars and Sorb-Apples

Beginning, deceptively, with a spontaneous casualness similar to *Peach*, the poem provides a major anticipation of those *Last Poems* which envisage death as a journey through the underworld of Greek myth. The tone is an unusual combination of religious meditation and intoxicated celebration. You might explore in this poem the virtuosity with which Lawrence transforms and reconciles apparent opposites. The pose of decadence with which the poem opens becomes a quest for pure self-hood; decay is envisaged as a process of purification.

Title **Medlars** small fruits resembling apples, eaten by sucking from their skins when brown and decayed.

  9 **muscat** grape variety yielding a strong, sweet white wine.

10 **Marsala** sherry-like wine from Sicily.

24 **wonderful... hellish** the oxymoron (a figure of speech which places together apparent opposites) is deliberately provocative. The hell in question is, of course, Hades, the underworld of Greek myth, not the Christian fiery pit.

25 **Orphic** Orpheus was a legendary Greek hero around whom cults arose. Orphic rites involved the eating of sacrifices associated with *Dionysos* (26) the Greek god of wine; their eventual object was to release the immortal soul from the body in which it was considered to be entombed.

29 **a new partner** the phrase combines two aspects: Orpheus entered the underworld to secure the return of his wife, Euridyce, from Pluto its God. But he lost her again by failing to observe the condition that he must not look back for her before

reaching daylight. Orphic beliefs held that the soul is incarnated in a succession of different bodies. The second idea predominates here.

38 **retorts**   vessels used for distillation and purification.

41 *Jamque vale*   (iamque vale) and now farewell! (Latin).

53 *ego sum*   I am (Latin).

54 *sono io*   I am – emphatic (Italian).

55 **Intoxication of final loneliness**   the soul to be reincarnated no further, finally achieves pure, disembodied separateness of being.

Almond Blossom

Joyful surprise at the winter blossoming of the almond tree stimulates this poetic improvisation on the idea of miraculous rebirth. The almond was once a symbol of resurrection. Stages in the story of Christ are engrafted with the symbolic possibilities of the tree's appearance and its blossom. The dead metallic-looking wood and the organic vitality of the flowers it puts forth lead Lawrence to hope for the end of the machine-age through which he felt the world was passing. As so often in his poetry, Lawrence seeks a sense of fulfilment by pushing the creative tension between opposites to a climax. (See Approaches p. 157 for more on Lawrence's interest in the crucifixion.)

11 **bitterness**   there are two kinds of almond tree, sweet and bitter,

21 **annunciation**   announcement, in the Christian calendar the angel Gabriel's revelation to the Virgin Mary that she is carrying Jesus.

31 **many-cicatrized**   a cicatrice is a scar.

37 **amphoras, craters...** etc.   Greek pots of various shapes.

45 **Sirius**   popularly known as the dog-star (see note on line 59).

46 **Gethsemane**   place where Jesus was betrayed by Judas and so, in a sense, where his crucifixion began.

48 **tree of life**   in the Bible, a fruit-bearing tree in the garden of Eden.

57 **naked tree of blossom**   the tree blossoms leafless, like Adam and Eve before they took up fig leaves, perhaps?

59 **dog-star**   Sirius, associated with excessive heat.

64 **epithalamion**   wedding song praising bride and groom.

91 **five times wide open**   the red flush at the centre of the white
flowers when open recalls the five wounds (stigmata) carried by
Jesus on the Cross, a reminder that rebirth can only be achieved
through suffering. The blossoms seem to surpass Christ in their
sixth opening (92). The red and white of the blossom also
symbolizes the union of body and spirit: *blood-consciousness* and
nerve-consciousness in Lawrence's terms.

The Mosquito

This mock ode moves from the disdainful civility of Lawrence's
address to the mosquito, *Monsieur* (2), to casual slaughter of the
insect as the poet avenges himself at the end of the poem. The idea
of addressing so eloquently a virtual *nothingness* is in itself comic.
The implicit contrast with the Romantic odes of the early
Nineteenth Century by Shelley and Keats, which reverently
apostrophize their subjects, adds to the amusement. Shelley's *To a
Skylark*, for example, begins in all seriousness: *Hail to thee, blithe
spirit!*

You might compare this poem with *Man and Bat*, also about the
limits of co-existence, and *Fish* which shows a different response to
a creature Lawrence has killed.

9 **Winged Victory**   statue of the goddess of victory, traditionally
equipped with wings.

65 **pæan**   chant of triumph, the high-pitched whine of the
mosquito.

Fish

The sinuous, darting movements of the lines and the alliterative
sibilance (*sluice of sensation along your sides*) convey the poet's
imaginative empathy with the life experience of the fish.
Recollected encounters with particular fish, however, reveal
differences from humans. Fish are creatures of a single element.
With no need to leave the womb and no love-life, they are
complete in themselves, requiring no 'other'. In comparison,
humans are latecomers to the world who are divided between the

elements, and because of their gender they can only struggle towards a singleness of being that the fish effortlessly retains.

20 **Even snakes lie together**   unlike fish, snakes copulate.
31 **Curvetting**   in the leap known as a curvet, a horse's hind legs kick out before the forelegs return to the ground.
122 *Fish are beyond me*   he admits he cannot know them fully. *Beyond*, a key word for Lawrence, combines throwaway colloquialism with philosophical exactness.
131 **lucent**   shining.
163 **Sulphur**   non-metallic element, associated with fire. Sun-loving creatures, Lawrence fancifully suggests, seek to redress an imbalance in their nature by consuming aquatic creatures.
171 **Jesus was called The Fish**   the fish was an obscure early Christian symbol for Jesus, but what connections, if any, is Lawrence making? In the Bible, water is the dominant element at the origin of the earth and at its destruction in the flood. Perhaps, like the fish, Jesus is a pure spirit at one with his element – except in the 'middle', presumably, when he experienced dividedness as a man. Perhaps, more provocatively, Lawrence suggests that Jesus is unknowable by him, just as fish are?

Man and Bat

Lawrence knows that he is amusingly conventional in his disgust for the bat. How does he reveal this in his self-portrayal in the poem? The attempt to apprehend its 'otherness' is limited to the essentially comic ending, a rare instance (as also in *Fish*), of Lawrence, imagining himself from the creature's point of view. In its form, like many of the free verse poems, it aims at the spontaneity of oral, performance poetry.

125 *a sghembo*   crookedly, obliquely (Italian).
139 **For I would have had to kill him if he'd bitten me**   you may recall the fate of the mosquito.
149 **pipistrello**   Italian for pipistrelle, a species of small bat.

Snake

Probably written in July 1920 in Taormina, Sicily, where Lawrence and Frieda lived for two years, this has become Lawrence's best-known poem. How effectively does the free verse bring together the physical presence of the snake and the man's self-questionings?

Though possibly drawing upon an actual encounter, Lawrence's interest in the snake's symbolism, religious and psychological, is evident in previous writings, for example:

> If there is a serpent of secret and shameful desire in my soul, let me not beat it out of my consciousness with sticks. Let me bring it to the fire to see what it is. For a serpent is a thing created... the snake must wreathe his way secretly along the path that belongs to him, and when I see him asleep in the sunshine I shall admire him in his place.

The Reality of Peace, 1917

A view of the snake as *one of the lords of life* (71) contrasts sharply with the role of the serpent in the Christian myth of Adam and Eve where the snake acts as an agent of the devil inducing the Fall of Man through sexual knowledge. The poem, with its tone of religious awe, reworks the mythical view of the snake in an attempt to come to terms with human sexuality. Acceptance, fascination, even worship, vie with fear, repression and disgust.

The *fissure* (7) from which the snake emerges, the *burning bowels* (20) from which it originates, and the man's revulsion at its penetration of the *horrid black hole* (52), together with the phallic suggestiveness of the snake itself, have, understandably, excited speculation over the precise physical and psychological implications of the poem. Such a reading though justifiable, can lead to too narrow an interpretation of a poem which seeks a more generalized acceptance of the darker aspects of human nature, through attention to the natural world in which man has yet to find an appropriate place. The snake has achieved its full potential as a life form moving freely above and below ground; the man, divided between the voice of education and his blood-instinct, is still struggling to fulfil himself. (For more on this poem see Approaches pp. 146–7)

The form of the poem has been likened to a short story. Do you find this a helpful comparison?

21 **Etna**   an active volcano, termed by the Greeks the Pedestal of

Heaven. Its closeness supports the snake's god-like status and the idea that he issues from some ancient creative source.

66 **the albatross** in *The Rime of the Ancient Mariner* (1798) by S. T. Coleridge, the Mariner offends nature by killing an albatross. He is released from a torment of isolation and thirst when he spontaneously responds to the beauty of some water-snakes.

Baby Tortoise

This is the first in a cycle of six poems in which Lawrence explores, with tragi-comic intent, connections between the evolutionary history of life on earth, the crucifixion of Christ, and the contradictory nature of human sexuality – all through the imagined life experience of a male tortoise. As a baby, in proud self-sufficiency, it thinks itself a lone voyager in the universe. Unlike human children, it is free from the constraints of parental love.

The remarkable status accorded the tortoise is not a private Lawrentian whim. In many African creation myths, stories about our origins like *Genesis* in the Bible, the tortoise takes a leading role. In this and the following poem, how well do you think the tortoise supports the extraordinary blend of Lawrence's views of it as pathetic, heroic, domestic, comic, tragic? (See Approaches pp. 146–7 for a comparison with *Snake*.)

55 **Ulysses** mythical hero (Odysseus in Greek myth) whose voyage of adventure is the subject of Homer's epic poem the *Odyssey*. The rowing motion of the tortoise's legs allows the comparison with an ancient oar-powered ship.

57 **Buon viaggio** have a good voyage! (Italian).

59 **Titan** one of a group of primitive Greek warrior gods, also used figuratively to describe someone of gigantic stature.

80 **Invincible fore-runner** two ideas combine here, one essentially mythical – the tortoise as the first form of life; the other to do with a particular theory of evolution according to which each individual recapitulates the prior development of the species. Together these ideas produce Lawrence's notion that the baby tortoise sees himself as the first creature on earth.

Tortoise Shout

This is the last in the cycle of six poems. The cry of the male tortoise at the moment of sexual climax echoes other involuntary animal utterances expressing extremes of feeling. The ambivalence (agony/ecstacy) of this most mysterious of cries offers insight into the tragedy of man's state: in sexual intercourse he suffers recognition of his dividedness so as to be made whole, just as Jesus was crucified into eternal life, Lawrence implies.

You may find the poem extravagant if you miss the absurdity and pathos which Lawrence communicates along with the tragedy by projecting the plight of all sexually divided creatures upon a tortoise. (See Approaches pp. 156–160 for more on Lawrence's treatment of sex.)

14 **plasm**   living matter.
19 **pæan**   song of praise, triumph, or gratitude.
25–26 **Why was the veil torn?... soul's torn membrane**   the sacred veil of the temple which ripped in two at the moment of Jesus' death is compared with a kind of spiritual male maidenhead.
36 **tupping**   copulating.
42 **Pentecost**   Christian festival commemorating the descent of the Holy Spirit upon the disciples after the Crucifixion.
85 **Osiris**   an ancient Egyptian god who was murdered by being torn to pieces. His wife, Isis, after a long search, recovered his remains.

Turkey-Cock

Associating the turkey's appearance and origins with the native peoples of North and South America (Red Indians, Aztecs) Lawrence is led to speculate that the cry of the bird might herald a new age in which pagan practices might be revived. Having built the poem to this crescendo and the turkey to the improbable status of the herald of apocalypse, Lawrence impishly suggests that the bird is merely an imperfect product of the furnace of creation – its dross-like coat a sign of impurity.

The poem was one of Lawrence's favourites. It is not hard to see why – it has the air of an extempore or live performance in which the preposterous mingles with the profound. Lawrence liked to bring off these improbable blends of feeling.

12 **wattles** the loose fleshy appendage on a turkey's head or throat. See also lines 29 and 88.

18 **mantilla** veil or cape (Spanish).

20 **dross** impurity– here the scum removed from smelted metal.

61 **Huichilobos** possibly a variant of Huitzilopochtli, the Aztec war-god of ancient Mexico, to whom blood sacrifices were made. Lawrence's novel *The Plumed Serpent* imagines, with approval, the reintroduction of Aztec cults to twentieth-century Mexico.

84 **Amerindians** native tribes of the American continent.

89 **jabot** frill on shirt.

Humming-Bird

It is now thought that this is the only poem Lawrence wrote about a creature that he knew only from books and not from life. Do you find the absence of direct apostrophe to the creature, so apparent in poems like *Turkey-Cock*, significant? The poem encapsulates a fanciful intuition about the humming-bird: that it is prehistoric in origin and seems too small for its pterodactyl-like behaviour.

Kangaroo

The peculiarity of Australia's wildlife, isolated from the rest of the animal kingdom for millenia, exercises Lawrence's imagination here. Despite the brief reference to aborigines, there is little philosophical or anthropomorphic extension of the initial insight. Contrast the poem with *Snake*, for example. It is a rarity in Lawrence's animal poetry in that it is an almost purely descriptive piece which evokes the earthy maternal gravity of the kangaroo. What do you think the poem gains and loses through this restriction of focus? (See Approaches pp. 147–8 for a discussion of anthropomorphism.)

11 **antipodal** from the antipodes, literally a region opposite to another: in Europe's case Australia.

Mountain Lion

Philip Hobsbaum has suggested (in *A Reader's Guide to D. H. Lawrence*) that this poem could be written out as prose without much loss, and that the paragraphs but not the line endings are important. It is a miniature short story, then, rather than a poem. It contains shifts of mood and a sequence of events rather than the shifts of tone and sudden leaps of thought of the most memorable of Lawrence's animal poems. Do you agree with Hobsbaum's judgement? (Task 6 on p. 173 provides a way to explore this issue across a range of Lawrence's poems.)

The callous dismissal of *a million or two of humans* (45) has caused readers dismay. Of course, Lawrence is making a controversial point about rarity and value, but is it too strident? At the centre of the poem is the vivid word-sketch of the lion's face which the poet refers back to in the closing lines.

  2 **balsam**   evergreen tree.
 16 ***Qué tiene, amigo?***   what have you got, my friend? (Spanish).
 17 **León**   lion (Spanish).
 31 **Hermoso es!**   it is beautiful (Spanish).

from *Pansies*

How Beastly the Bourgeois Is

To what extent do you find the sour satire of this poem enlivened by the use of various tones of voice – affected, slangy, lecturing, irascible, mocking? Experiment by reading the poem aloud in different ways. What ideas and attitudes do you find expressed in the mushroom/fungus/toadstool similes?

  1 **bourgeois**   a member of the middle-class. The word is often used pejoratively, as here, to suggest narrow-mindedness, complacency, and conventionality.

When I Went to the Circus

Some contemporary attitudes to circuses might lead to a misreading of this poem. Is it the animals or the audience that Lawrence regards as captive and diminished?

27 **ammonites** a fossil resembling a coiled elephant's trunk.

49 **flat personalities in two dimensions** a companion poem, *When I Went to the Film*, ends:

> It was like being in heaven, which I am sure has
>   a white atmosphere
> upon which shadows of people, pure personalities
> are cast in black and white, and move
> in flat ecstasy, supremely unfelt,
> and heavenly.

Lawrence prefers the vivid if occasionally tawdry reality of the circus to the superficial fantasy-ideals of the movies – black-and-white and silent, of course, in his day.

Whatever Man Makes

What implicit contrast does the poem make between native crafts and mass-produced consumer goods?

3 **Hindu** a follower of Hinduism, the main religious system in India.

4 **Navajo** North American indian tribe.

The Elephant is Slow to Mate

This happy celebration of the elephants' mating presents these animals as experts in the blood rhythms of sex. How skilful and appropriate do you find the use of rhyme and rhythm here? (See Approaches pp. 157–160 for more on Lawrence's treatment of sex.)

The Mess of Love

For a discussion of what Lawrence called *sex-in-the-head* see Approaches p. 157.

11 **immortelle** French for immortal; here, a dried flower, often used to adorn a grave.

Red-Herring

The title itself, given its common meaning of a misleading clue, may prove confusing. The old saying 'Neither fish nor fowl but plain red-herring' indicates that a red-herring can also be something which lies between two categories into which it does not fit. The poem is an autobiographical skit. (See Approaches pp. 150–4 and the Chronology p.167 for more on Lawrence's background.)

To Women, as Far as I'm Concerned

See Approaches pp. 149–150 for an activity based on this poem.

Desire is Dead

See Approaches p. 161 for a discussion of the tree symbol in Lawrence's poetry.

Wages

Work, the poem argues, has become devalued by too close an association with money. The poem negatively anticipates a modern, acquisitive consumer society. A comparison with *Whatever Man Makes* (p. 82) suggests what Lawrence feels has been lost.

Relativity

This poem refers to Einstein's theory of relativity, a view of the universe based on the principle that all motion is relative, which undermined commonsense distinctions between space and time. See Chronology p. 167 for the date of this theory.

The Triumph of the Machine

The title is highly ironic and expresses Lawrence's scepticism about the power of machines to liberate. In Chapter 17 of *Women in Love*, modern industrial methods are seen as:

the destruction of the organic purpose, the organic unity, and the subordination of every organic unit to the great mechanical purpose.

What values does Lawrence assert in this poem, as nature takes its gleeful revenge?

    4 **acanthus** a kind of prickly-leafed plant.

For a Moment

Lawrence often felt that people were most splendidly godlike when least self-conscious. The tram-conductor, the girl with the washing, his wife Frieda, and the bookish Italian are supremely unaware of the moments of self-transcendence the poet glimpses. Another *pansy* provides a warning footnote:

Men Like Gods
When men think they are like gods
they are usually much less than men
being conceited fools

    4 **Hyacinthus** a beautiful Spartan prince – loved by the gods Apollo and Zephyrus, killed in a jealous dispute between them.
    9 **Io** a princess of Argos, she was pursued by the god Zeus and subsequently driven into restless flight by his jealous wife, Hera.
        Danaë mother of the hero Perseus by Zeus, who visited her in a shower of gold when her father imprisoned her. Lawrence seems to think there is more than one Danaë and may be confusing her with the Danaides, who were punished in Hades by being forced to pour water into a sieve for eternity.
  14 **Isis** Egyptian goddess of the earth and moon and wife of *Osiris*; she quested long but triumphantly for the dismembered body of her murdered husband.
  17 **Centaur** half-man (down to the loins), half-horse, the centaurs lived a wild and savage life. One of them, Chiron, had a reputation for wisdom.

Thought

Lawrence saw orthodox, scientific, rational thought as superficial and life-denying, a function of the nerves and the brain only. He sought to restore wholeness of being by emphasizing the *blood-*

consciousness of the body.

You could compare the effectiveness of the poem in communicating this idea with that of a famous declaration of faith Lawrence made in a letter to Ernest Collings in 1913:

> My great religion is a belief in the blood, the flesh as being wiser than the intellect. We can go wrong with our minds, but what our blood feels and believes and says is always true.

See Approaches pp. 160–1 for more on Lawrence's philosophy.

from *Last Poems*

Middle of the World

Lawrence was in the final year of his life and living in the South of France when he wrote this fresh, serene poem. He wrote in a letter:

> I lie in bed and look at the islands out to sea, and think of the Greeks...

The sea is, of course, the Mediterranean which gives the poem its title, and which is often seen as the setting for the dawn of civilization.

4 **Dionysos** the youthful god of wine whose final exploit occurred aboard a ship on which he was being taken as a slave. He metamorphosed himself into a lion, the mast into a serpent, and the sailors into dolphins. Foliage grew up around the vessel. The story thus happily brings together some of Lawrence's favourite symbols.

8 **Minoan distance** i.e. between mainland Greece and the island of Crete, former realm of King Minos.

13 **Cnossos** capital city of Crete under King Minos.

17 **Tiryns** one of the most ancient towns in Greece, its excavation towards the end of the Nineteenth century revealed much about legendary heroes.

Red Geranium and Godly Mignonette

God is imagined as a romantic artist of the Lawrentian kind, creating the world to meet his own spontaneous emotional need rather than according to a divine plan. The poem is a playful attack upon the philosophical doctrine of Platonic idealism according to which all objects in the world are merely imperfect imitations of their ideal forms which exist in the mind of God. Characteristically, Lawrence prizes the actual above the ideal. How successfully does his use of a teasing, colloquial tone and sensuous detail, animate an essentially abstract argument?

> 5 **mignonette** delicately formed plant, grown for its fragrance.
> 9 **heliotrope** literally a plant which turns its flowers and leaves to follow the sun; here specifically a fragrant herb with small purple flowers.

The Man of Tyre

The Greek philosopher's abstract thought and his drift towards monotheism – the belief that there is only one God – are arrested by his sighting of a woman who incarnates Aphrodite. What difference is made to the poem by our knowledge that she is an ordinary woman? Perhaps the suggestion is that polytheism – belief in many gods – and monotheism are both merely ideas, but that the former has the greater capacity to allow for transcendent experiences of reality. *For A Moment* (p. 89) may provide you with a helpful comparison. You may feel that the joke, a gentle one, is at the expense of all philosophizing: the Greek misses the *message to the man* (15) and contemplates rather than acts.

The painterly rendering of the woman's body and the blend of humour and reverence offered by the poem, are worth exploring. For Lawrence the woman is real, not an idealized work of art.

> 1 **The man of Tyre** Maximus of Tyre (c. AD 125–185), a philosopher who held that *the human form in its perfection is the nearest of all things to God*, especially as interpreted in fine sculpture.
> 19 **Aphrodite** Greek goddess of love and beauty (Venus to the Romans) she was believed to have arisen from the foam of the sea, and was the subject of many sculptures and paintings.

Whales Weep Not!

Comparisons with *Fish* (p. 47), *The Elephant is Slow to Mate* (p.82), and *Tortoise Shout* (p. 65) are invited by this poem. The mammalian whales and dolphins, unlike the cold-blooded fish, conduct a deeply satisfying love-life. The whales' copulation is described in radiantly religious terms (Christian and pagan) and the poem concludes with the appearance of Lawrence's own sacred symbol of peace and fulfilment: the rainbow.

The mating of these creatures reconciles many of the familiar Lawrentian opposites: heat and cold, fire and water, male and female, power and tenderness. The movement is one of surging celebration to which the piling up of clauses beginning with *And* – a major stylistic feature of the Bible – imparts a feeling of worship. (See Approaches pp. 156–7 for more on the relationship between Lawrence's sexual and religious thinking.)

12 **bull**   male whale obviously, but with perhaps a glance at Zeus, the greatest of Greek gods, who assumed the appearance of a bull in some of his amorous excursions from Mount Olympus.

21 **Cherubim**   and...

28 **Seraphim**   The whales are seen as Gods in their heaven attended by archangels who participate in the bliss of their love-making. Traditionally, *Seraphim* are depicted as red and fiery and associated with love, and *Cherubim* are associated with knowledge.

25 **waters of the beginning and the end**   see the end of *Fish* (p. 47 and note on pp. 119–120)

Invocation to the Moon

In Lawrence's personal system of thought the sun and moon were opposed principles of the universe between which it was necessary to find a balance:

> ...the sun, like a lion, loves the bright red blood of life, and can give it infinite enrichment if we know how to receive it ... and the cool, bright ever varying moon ... is she who would caress our nerves...

> *Apocalypse*

In much of his writing the power of the moon – often seen as a devouring female – is resisted. See for example, Chapter 19 of *Women in Love*. Here instead Lawrence seeks reconciliation. The moon is a noble mother figure who, after the spirit has journeyed through the houses of the heavens after death, restores the spirit to a healed body. The ending of *The Ship of Death* (p. 99) also envisages a rebirth in the flesh. (See Approaches p. 152 for comment on an autobiographical element in this poem.)

Title **Invocation** the act of calling upon a deity for favour, often through incantation or prayer.
12 **Villa of Venus** dwelling place of the goddess of physical love.
14 **six** together with the moon, the seven heavenly rulers over the earth: Mercury, Mars, Venus, Jupiter, Saturn and the sun (Pluto, Uranus, and Neptune do not figure).
16 **far-off lingering lady** Venus.
17 **lion with golden paws** Lawrence's frequently used emblem for the sun.
19 **silver bells... cockleshells** the reference to the nursery rhyme *Mary Mary Quite Contrary* gives the poem a whimsical air suggestive of a child-like return to the mother.

Bavarian Gentians

See Approaches pp. 162–6 for a detailed activity, and discussion of this carefully crafted poem.

2 **Michaelmas** specifically 29th September, Feast of St Michael, but often used, as here, to mean Autumn.
4 **Pluto's gloom** Pluto was another name for the god of the underworld, Hades.
8 **Dis** a further name for the underworld and Pluto himself.
9 **Demeter** goddess of agriculture and harvest (Ceres to the Romans) sometimes represented as holding a torch. In contrast, the poet, wishing to enter the darkness rather than illuminate it, chooses the deep blue gentian to show him the way.
14 **Persephone** daughter of Demeter and Zeus, Pluto carried her off to the underworld as his bride. Demeter, in protest at Zeus having allowed this, refused to produce any crops. A compromise was reached by which Persephone spent two thirds of the year above ground and one third in the underworld.

Originally a fertility myth to explain the seasonal nature of crops, the story became associated in later cults with the burial of the body and the immortality of the soul.

In the Cities

In ancient cities the dead were as if alive, gentle presences in the pure air; in modern cities the living are as if dead, oppressed by the exhalations of the polluted air. It is a poem about the weight of history, the relationship of past to present and not simply about ecology.

6 **miasma**   fog of noxious vapours.
13 **Mycenae**   ancient Greek city of which many remains, including the Lion Gate, survive.
19 **bursten**   burst open, as from excess, or like a boil.

The Ship of Death

Lawrence's life from the age of 26 onwards had been shaped by travel and the various ideas of journeying which lend it religious purpose: a pilgrimage in search of ancient gods; a quest for wholeness and peace; and now, finally, the voyage in the dark.

This is his most far-reaching exploration of the death experience in its speculation about the eventual return of the soul to its body. Much reworked early versions of the poem envisage merely peace, oblivion and, obscurely, a continuing voyage of the soul. Death is, however, consistently seen as a long mysterious process in which the division of death from life is imperceptible. Readers sometimes find the conclusion willed, fanciful, and unspecific. What do you feel Lawrence means: a Christian resurrection, a pagan transmigration of souls? Characteristically, Lawrence's version of death deliberately avoids adherence to a specific doctrine. Do you think this matters?

3–4 **apples falling... exit from themselves**   see *Medlars and Sorb-Apples* (p. 38) for an earlier use of autumnal fruit to explore the fate of the soul upon its release from the body.
8 **ship of death**   Lawrence was taken with the ancient Etruscan custom of burying a small bronze ship with their dead. Other ancient cultures, e.g. the Vikings, Egyptians, actually buried kings in ships or tombs meticulously provisioned for long journeys, as

in Section VII of the poem. An early version describes the souls of those lacking the spiritual discipline to build their own ships of death stranded on the banks of the rivers of the underworld, awaiting Charon the ferryman to take them across.

17–18 **...And his own quietus make/with a bare bodkin?** the lines include a quotation, from the famous speech on suicide in Shakespeare's play, *Hamlet* (Act III Scene 1), meaning 'can a man achieve a peaceful release from life with just a dagger?' To die well, the poem implies, requires careful spiritual preparation. Some readers have considered the lines on suicide a digression which weakens the poem. Do you agree?

38 **ark** Lawrence's eclectically constructed ship now resembles the ark in which Noah survived the biblical flood.

Shadows

The reverent poise of this poem is remarkable. Its movement is utterly persuasive though its only obvious structural principle is the thrice repeated *And if ...* finally answered by *then*. *Bavarian Gentians* and *The Ship of Death* may seem, by comparison, almost over-reliant on imagery to achieve their sense of mystery. Here, flowering and decay, the phases of the moon, Autumn descending into winter, falling asleep and awaking, oblivion and renewal seem more directly expressive of the experiences of mind and body in the reality of dying. In contrast, the other poems use imagery to strain beyond what is known, daring to seek acceptable imaginative anticipations.

It is interesting that Lawrence refers to a single God here rather than the multiple gods of many of the other late poems. Perhaps he had to find ways of making peace with the various aspects of his religious imagination. Are orthodoxy and consistency beside the point here? You could argue that the adequacy of myths in poetry rests not in our submission to their doctrinal authority but in their imaginative faithfulness to the experience of the moment.

16 **singing darker than the nightingale** the poem distantly echoes Keats' *Ode to a Nightingale* in which the poet, afflicted with melancholy, longs for oblivion, being *half in love with easeful death.*

Approaches

Approaches Through Poetic Form

D. H. Lawrence was certainly a prolific writer. Most read for his novels, novellas and stories, he also wrote travel books, plays, highly idiosyncratic works of philosophy, psychology and literary criticism, as well as various essays, and poetry. Towards the end of his life he exhibited some of his paintings. Compulsively original and highly suspicious of conventional ideas, especially to do with religion, sex, and art, he developed a questioning attitude to the modern world as it emerged in the first three decades of the Twentieth century. Whilst contributing to a post-Victorian climate of greater openness concerning sexuality and the life of the body, he was hostile to mechanization and what he saw as modern posturing through intellectual sophistication; they diminished a sacred sense of the life-force naturally expressed through human beings and other living creatures.

At times, Lawrence directed his creative energy towards one type of writing; at others, he worked simultaneously across several, reaching out through his thoughts and feelings for new and appropriate forms. The resulting continuities in idea and expression between these different forms have sometimes led to the poetry being mistakenly regarded as a mere by-product of the fiction. Certainly, some of the early poems parallel scenes in the novels, particularly from the semi-autobiographical *Sons and Lovers*. Comparisons here are of interest, and notes to individual poems indicate where to find complementary prose passages. However, the wider critical issue when making such comparisons is essentially one of form rather than of subject-matter. Some passages of Lawrence's prose have the rhythmic repetitions and rich diction of poetry, while some of his poems, if their verse breaks were abandoned for paragraphs, would be indistinguishable from prose. Recognition of Lawrence as one of the finest and most original poets of the century has been impeded, even though free verse has become an accepted and much used form, by anxieties as to whether he wrote much real poetry at all.

This merging and blurring of forms did not worry Lawrence. If, as he believed, people in the modern world were losing touch with their emotional and physical lives, and so with a full sense of their place in the universe – Lawrence liked to think in cosmic terms – then ways of thinking and restrictive forms of poetic expression needed to be changed. Writing was for Lawrence a part of life and a means of discovering and affirming how best to live it; only incidentally was art concerned with the creation of objects – beautiful, complete, separate, finished. He aimed to write poetry which would achieve an effect of spontaneous immediacy, giving voice to aspects of the self which might otherwise be repressed, and so letting the fresh air of informality into what had become the rather stuffy closed room of late-Victorian poetic good manners. Poetry could, he believed, benefit by moving closer to prose and to various kinds of speech, whether this be through the casualness of conversation, the urgency of emotional outburst or the vigour of dialect forms.

Metre and Free Verse

Central to any understanding of form in Lawrence's poetry is the distinction between verse in **metre**, where lines of poetry repeat patterns of stressed and unstressed syllables with greater regularity than is usually found in spoken English, and **free verse**, where regularity of metre and rhyme is given up. Rhythm and the sounds of words remain very important in free verse, as they are in any expressive use of language, but they do not keep to regular patterns of repetition. To give some idea of what Lawrence was trying to get away from in his poetry, it is worth looking at a very early poem of his, one he once thought *a little masterpiece*:

Flapper

Love has crept out of her sealèd heart
    As a field-bee, black and amber,
    Breaks from the winter-cell, to clamber
Up the warm grass where the sunbeams start.

Mischief has come in her dawning eyes,
    And a glint of coloured iris brings

Such as lies along the folded wings
Of the bee before he flies.

Who, with a ruffling, careful breath,
    Has opened the wings of the wild young sprite?   10
    Has fluttered her spirit to stumbling flight
In her eyes, as a young bee stumbleth?

Love makes the burden of her voice.
    The hum of his heavy, staggering wings
    Sets quivering with wisdom the common things
That she says, and her words rejoice.

The concern to maintain the metre here, basically a four stress line with a three stress line for a sense of finality at the end of stanzas two and four, is also evident from the stressed syllable mark (Lawrence's) on the end of *sealèd* in line 1. This pattern leads to awkward linking phrases, at the start of line 7, for instance. There is also an obvious preoccupation with the sound-patterning of words – see, for example, the alliteration (marked repetition of consonants) in lines 10 and 14. There is also the use of an old-fashioned verb form (*stumbleth* in line 12) to serve the dual purpose of making the piece sound more 'poetical' and helping the rhyme scheme along. The overall effect is that readers are more aware of the poet's attempt to keep up the regular metre, other sound effects, and rhyme scheme, than they are of the actual subject and emotion of the poem itself. The poet may well have lost sight of these as well. *Compositions*, the mature Lawrence's scornful term for such poems, is apt in its suggestion of a forced exercise.

If you compare this poem with *The Wild Common* (p. 2) where varied and often extended line lengths allow a much looser approach to rhythm, and *After the Opera* (p. 12) where all attempts at metre, but not significant rhythm or rhyme, are abandoned, you will begin to see what Lawrence gained by moving towards free verse in much of his poetry.

However, a concept of poetry committed to self-expression and an effect of immediacy is not without its problems. While the writer may release feelings and gain satisfaction from this, communication of these to the reader may not always be successful. Naked expressions of emotion can be embarrassing or unaffecting, particularly if the poem does not convey sufficiently the context of the experience being portrayed. A poem may be true to the personal impulse of the moment but will it engage the reader's imagination and so transcend the occasion from which it originates? It may, after all, be easier to escape the limitations of a pre-conceived form than to invent a new one which is both faithful to the experience and rich enough in its language to hold the attention through repeated readings. If a free-verse poem fails to convince readers that its form is *necessary* rather than random and diffuse, it will be seen as an artistic failure: self-indulgent, and lacking in most of the expressive resources of poetry. Lawrence, however, moved gradually towards the writing of free verse, and continued to use other forms later in his life. The following survey of his main groups of poems will reveal the remarkable variety of Lawrence's experiments with form and the ideas about poetry and art which developed alongside them.

For many readers, Lawrence's poetry has been represented by a few much anthologized poems, among them *Piano, Snake, Bavarian Gentians* and a bunch of *Pansies*. So it may come as a surprise to discover that he published ten volumes of poetry, more than most writers known for their poetry alone, and that his *Complete Poems* includes over 1,000 different pieces as well as a number of variant versions. This selection aims to include those that are agreed to be his best poems whilst also suggesting something of Lawrence's range through examples of his work which test the limits of what poetry can be. The poems are generally arranged according to Lawrence's own classifications, though it must be mentioned that he did regroup, and revise his work for different editions. For early versions of *Bavarian Gentians* and *Piano* see p. 163 and p. 172.

Early Poems: The Young Man and the Demon

The poems in this section embrace various lyrical expressions of emotion concerning childhood anxieties, sexual awakening, struggles towards independence, nostalgia and bereavement. In terms of their form, you will notice that these poems often rhyme regularly, though a particular rhyme scheme is rarely repeated in another poem. However, beneath the appearance of regular metre induced by the pattern of the lines on the page, you will find, if you experiment with reading the poems aloud, a resistance against settling for too regular a rhythm. An important critical issue for you to consider here is whether rhythmic awkwardness is a purposeful creative departure from a pattern, or merely an unsuccessful attempt to observe one. Opinions on this issue do differ, but you may well find that *Piano* (p. 1) and *The Bride* (p. 13), for example, provide instances of the former, while *The Wild Common*, which we are about to look at in some detail, provides instances of the latter.

When preparing his poems for the collected edition of 1928, two years before his death, Lawrence detected in his early work a struggle between a self-conscious, awkward, imitative versifier – the *young man* – and a spontaneous, authentic inner voice – the *demon*. Accordingly, he divided his poems into two categories: *rhyming poems*, the early work in which the young man, he felt, could be found nervously placing *his hand over the demon's mouth*, and the mature work in which the demon was allowed his uncensored say. He thus subversively associated verse in rhyme with inexperience, lack of originality and repression, and free verse with experience, originality and openness. The distinction offers an unusual way of looking at the role of rhyme. In this selection, all the poems in the *Early Poems* section, with the exception of *The Chief Mystery* were grouped under the *Rhyming Poems* heading. The remaining poems in this selection were placed in the *Unrhyming Poems* section, which, you will be quick to observe, anomalously contains quite a few poems with regular rhyme schemes as well as many occasional rhymes.

Activity

Read *The Wild Common* (p. 2) In what ways does it seem to you to embody a struggle between the *young man* and the *demon*? Do you find Lawrence's distinction a helpful one?

Discussion

You may consider the demon strongly present here in the sharpness of observation (e.g. the gorse bushes, the rabbits), the surprising vigour of many of the verbs, the sensual play of wind and water, and the frank celebration of physical experience. It is perhaps the fifth stanza which lets the demon down. Apart from the urgency of the *pulsing waters,* (18) the poeticism of the rhetorical questions in lines 17 and 18 is fatuous and contributes to the unfocused, derivative-sounding effect. The use of *embossed* (19) to achieve the required rhyme is awkward despite the enjambment which carries the emphasis over onto *Withered* (20). *Proclaim* (4) at the end of the first stanza is, perhaps, similarly grandiose though it does have some justification in the image of the peewits as *lords*.

Nevertheless, this activity may have raised doubts over the ease with which Lawrence's distinction can be applied. These would be well-founded. Highly noticeable rhymes are not necessarily the result of an attempt to silence the demon. They are more likely to be a clumsy response to the requirements of rhyming. The poem is momentarily precious, after the manner of Rossetti or Swinburne, and at times vague. While being unusually open about youthful auto-eroticism, the desire for this open utterance can lead to poor expression, for example in line 24, as easily as the verse form does.

Interestingly, when Lawrence later revised the poem, supposedly to *let the demon have his say*, it was extended but not improved. Whilst some of the most slackly 'poetic' lines, like those mentioned above, were excised, some banal rhymes and laboured explanations were added. The older man, rewriting the work of the younger, was not necessarily a better channel for the demon, particularly when the poem, as here, so intimately concerns a young man's experience. In recognition of this, the poems gathered under the heading *Early Poems* in this selection appear in their original versions which most critics now prefer.

In the end, the most revealing tension in the poem is not psychological but formal: that between the pull towards irregular line lengths and looser rhythms, and the attempt to hold differing line lengths within a regular pattern.

If you have begun to question Lawrence's ability to handle rhyme and metre, as many readers have, look at his work in the dialect ballad form, for example in *A Collier's Wife* (p.6), *Violets* (p.8), and *Whether or Not* (p. 14). Lawrence's skill with this form was much admired by Ezra Pound, a contemporary poet with a very fierce ear for poetic craftsmanship. Traditionally, the ballad metre employs a rough four beat line – sometimes alternating with a three beat line for variety and a sharpening of emphasis – in a four line stanza. The rhyme scheme is generally abcb.

Activity

Whether Or Not (p. 14) is a dialect ballad for different voices incorporating extensive exchanges in dialogue. Try reading the poem aloud, if possible in a group with each person taking a different part. How effective do you find the characterization? How successful is the poem in sustaining regular patterns of rhyme and rhythm whilst conveying idiomatic speech? Choose a stanza which seems to do this with particular clarity.

Discussion

For detailed comments on characterization and the handling of form refer to the Notes on pp. 110–111. One specific example of Lawrence's ability to combine a balanced scheme of rhyme and rhythm with natural speech patterns comes in the following tart exchange:

> You knowed as I was courtin' Tim Merfin.
> — Yis, I knowed 'e wor courtin' thee.
> An' yet you've been carryin' on wi' him.
> — Ay, an' 'im wi' me.   (157–160)

There is a keen sense of two characters in conflict. Lizzie Stainwright is accusatory in her tone while Widow Naylor pointedly reverses the emphasis in her final statement to deflate the argument. Clearly, the distancing from direct personal emotion enforced by the fictional elements of characterization, dialogue, and story allowed Lawrence to observe the requirements of a set stanza form. Perhaps, also, given his working-class and regional origins, the opportunity to use non-standard English was in itself a sufficiently enlivening release from this kind of formal observance. Similarly, *Ballad of Another Ophelia* (p. 22), which is also distanced from the immediately personal through the use of a characterized *persona*, is equally as at ease with rhyme and metre.

You may wonder what advantages the dialect ballad has over the short story, other than a pithy brevity and rhythmic momentum. There are two related points which answer this question. First, the ballad

141

draws upon an oral, folk tradition of popular narrative poetry and song and so provides a seemingly natural outlet for the voices of its characters. Secondly, in a short story or novel, dialogue in dialect can seem outlandishly quaint when, as almost invariably, it is juxtaposed with the Standard English of the narration.

Early Poems also provides in *After the Opera* (p. 12), with its delicate precision, and *The Chief Mystery* (p. 24), with its expansively ritualistic language, anticipations of different kinds of free verse to come. It would be misleading to suggest that Lawrence's best work is to be found only in the fictional, or free verse poems. In *Piano* (p. 1) and *The Bride* (p. 13), for example, the personal emotions are very strong and openly admitted, and pull against the underlying structure of the poems. Yet in each case they are objectified: through precise observation in the first, and the astonishingly beautiful closing image of the second. Of course, like all such critical assertions, this will need testing against your own experience of these poems.

Look! We Have Come Through!
Poetry of the Immediate Present

It is this group of poems that is most closely associated with Lawrence's use of free verse to explore a particular phase of his personal life. A general definition of free verse is offered on pp. 136–8. In prose, lineation (the setting out of words in lines) is random, a mere filling of the page between the margins. In free verse, lineation has great scope for differences in the length of adjacent lines – as in *Craving for Spring* (p. 32) or *Snake* (p. 59), for example – making it potentially a very expressive and dynamic form. Lawrence, for whom it was not a matter of classification, but of a fresh apprehension of the full reality of the lived moment, would have found such an academic definition of free verse dull. Here is his own, or a part of it:

> direct utterance from the instant, whole man. It is the soul and the
> mind and the body surging at once, nothing left out. They speak all

together. There is some confusion, some discord. But the confusion and the discord only belong to the reality as noise belongs to the plunge of water. It is no use inventing fancy laws for free verse, no use drawing a melodic line which all feet must toe... Whitman pruned away his clichés – perhaps his clichés of rhythm as of phrase. And this is about all we can do, deliberately, with free verse. We can get rid of the stereotyped movements and the old hackneyed associations of sound or sense.

(Poetry of the Present, 1919)

Walt Whitman was a major nineteenth-century American poet and a pioneer of free verse. His writing was influential on Lawrence although much of his work in the form was either more conversationally casual or descriptively exact than Whitman's which tended towards the rhetorical and grandiloquent. Of the poems included here, only *Craving for Spring* (p. 32) and to a lesser degree *Song of a Man Who Has Come Through* (p. 31) could be termed Whitmanesque. (See Task 12 on p. 175 for an opportunity to compare the style of Whitman's poetry with Lawrence's.)

Activity

What do you find most interesting in Lawrence's definition of free verse? Do you see any areas of difficulty or contradiction in the terms he uses? To what extent do you think the definition is relevant to the poems in *Look! We Have Come Through!* ? It is taken from an essay which Lawrence felt would have made a good preface to that volume.

Discussion

The definition is a kind of manifesto declaration. Free verse, Lawrence argues, is an attempt to express what it feels like to be fully alive in the present moment. In allowing simultaneous expression from different aspects of the self it is at once an expression of faith in the idea of the *whole man* and, in the acknowledgement of discord, a recognition of his dividedness. There is an implicit attack upon an obsession with *melody* in poetry and an attempted vindication of discordance. You might find a parallel here with the development of atonal music, by composers such as Schoenberg, in the early Twentieth-century. What in other types of poetry would be dismissed as flaws can be seen as potential signs of authenticity. Even the best verse in metre, referred to elsewhere in the essay as *the treasured gem-like lyrics of Shelley and Keats*, which aimed to express particular movements of feeling, falsified these in the very act of trying to preserve them. The perfection of form, in its state of balanced completion, was a misrepresentation of the essentially unfinished quality of the experience of the moment.

However rousing this declaration is, it is also conceptually fraught. Lawrence initially appears to be advocating the automatic writing of poetry, but there is ambiguity as to whether the poems are to be *written* spontaneously or whether they are to be worked over so as to achieve an *impression* of spontaneity. Later, there is a recognition that such writing as is envisaged could throw up a fair amount of cliché – the first phrase to come to mind is by no means always the freshest – and that the artist will have to revise to get rid of it.

In the *Look! We Have Come Through!* poems, free verse spans a range from the intimately minimal *Bei Hennef* (p.26) to the rhapsodic *Craving for Spring* (p.32); both express the urgency and incompleteness of the present moment. You may notice, however, that many of these poems make use of rhyme and sometimes metre. It is worth asking yourself whether this is arbitrary or whether in each case the theme links form with feeling. For example, the free verse *Gloire de Dijon* (p. 28) attempts a quick sketch which captures the play of light and water over the moving body of the woman, whilst also conveying the tender appreciativeness of the man's gaze: occasional feminine para-rhymes – *watch her/catch her* (2, 4) *glows as/roses* (7, 10) – and the image of the rose provide sufficient poise without loss of spontaneity. In contrast, the return to regular rhyme in *Roses on the Breakfast Table* (p. 28), lightened by the flow of enjambment, may contribute to the sense of personal wholeness, of a balanced acceptance of oneself, to set against the more conventional association of roses with transience, which the poem also accepts.

Meeting Among the Mountains (p. 29) shows a full commitment to rhyme and metre, perhaps as a means of controlling a sense of guilt that might otherwise prove overwhelming, while *A Young Wife* (p. 27), in using rhyme but not metre conveys the character's spellbound fascination with her husband combined with her direct admissions of anguish.

Three further questions are worth considering here. First, do the poems in *Look! We Have Come Through!* hold the reader's attention imaginatively rather than merely sympathetically, – the attention one might give to a friend speaking about personal matters – to allow them to survive the transition from the private to the public domain? Bertrand Russell, the philosopher and sometime friend of Lawrence, was provoked to callous indifference by the volume: *They may have come through, but I don't see why I should look.* Secondly, free verse poetry of this kind may require a particular kind of reading in which more attention needs to be paid to the flow of feeling and the sense of movement, and less to the scrutiny of individual words or phrases for complexity of meaning. Finally, is free verse necessarily best suited to a sense of the present and to the articulation of inner states? The next group of poems will help to provide some answers.

Birds, Beasts and Flowers: Acts of Attention

In this group, the commitment to free verse is total. The phrase 'acts of attention' was coined by the critic, Sandra Gilbert, out of one of Lawrence's remarks (see Approaches pp. 160–1) insisting on the importance of a fresh vision:

> The essential quality of poetry is that it makes a new effort of attention, and 'discovers' a new world within the known world.

It seems a particularly apt description of the poems in *Birds, Beasts and Flowers*, which often achieve their form through the context of an encounter, sometimes specific and in the flesh, sometimes imaginary, between Lawrence and a particular living thing. Many of the poems can be likened to the work of a painter: some the brief sketches of things observed; others, more fully contemplated, yielding a richly coloured painting. A further dimension is given by their sense of movement. This may rise from the behaviour of a creature itself, from interaction between Lawrence and the thing observed, from the process of apprehension as the eye is drawn to certain details or from the imaginative act in which different levels of the poet's inner self are brought to light.

In the history of literature animals have frequently been used as subjects, often with a moral purpose involving scant interest in the full reality of the creature itself. *Aesop's Fables,* for example, tend to abstract single animal characteristics. In the case of the tortoise and the hare, the slowness of the one and the quickness of the other are given moral values – modest persistence triumphs over proud and rash hastiness. Mediaeval treatises called bestiaries drew a Christian message from each story about a particular animal. These were often illustrated by an illuminated miniature of the creature in question. Lawrence draws upon this tradition; *Birds, Beasts and Flowers* can be seen as a deliberate attempt to create a modern bestiary, a menagerie of living emblems in which due respect is shown to the natural reality of creatures. They remain nonetheless capable of playing symbolic roles in new myths or parables. Sometimes Lawrence's animal poems draw conventionally upon the popular image of a creature in myth or folklore; in *Man and Bat* (p. 53), for instance. At others, they run counter to received ideas, including those of Lawrence himself.

Just as the 'fictional' poems provide a set of objective circumstances through which Lawrence finds release from an excessive concentration on inward personal experience, so the 'objects of attention' provide an external point of reference. Indeed, they can also serve as points of reference for the reader, since most will be known to them through direct experience or other literary representations. Do you find Lawrence's observation accurate and does the linguistic inventiveness with which it is rendered enable you to imagine the thing afresh? Whatever direction the poet's thoughts finally take, the quality of these poems depends on the extent to which the object's symbolic significance persuasively originates in the apprehension of its actual characteristics.

Activity

Compare the ways in which *Snake* (p. 59) and *Baby Tortoise* (p. 62) establish connections between physical observations and ideas.

Discussion

Snake takes the form of a narrative account of a purportedly chance encounter with this creature. Admiration for its poise and smoothness of movement is hypnotically conveyed by flowingly extended poetic lines with commas delicately deployed to mimic a change, or pause, in the movement. A contrast is established between the assured behaviour of the snake and the inner agitation of the poet, and this comes to be what the poem is about. The sequence of events and emotions – awed surprise, fascination, fear, inner conflict, aggression, guilt, and a final sense of unworthiness – enact a psychological parable about the dividedness of humans and the wholeness of snakes. It provides an instinctive corrective to the general cultural prejudice against snakes and the association with its role as the devil's agent in the Eden myth. (For more detailed notes on this poem see pp. 120–2.)

Baby Tortoise (p. 62) has a slight narrative element in the idea of the creature's epic first voyage across the garden, but unlike *Snake* it is not cast as a specific encounter. The dominant form is that of a sustained apostrophe, conventional in odes to animals, in which the creature is directly addressed in the second person: *You... your...* This form is adopted in most of the animal poems in this group – even in *Medlars and Sorb-Apples* (p. 38). There is frequently a comic edge which enlivens Lawrence's use of this rather old-fashioned mode. It is interesting, then, that he never feels sufficiently at ease with the snake to pretend to speak to it directly; from the outset the snake is specific and real, rather than an imaginative amalgam as most of the other animals are.

Many of the comparisons in *Baby Tortoise* would seem extravagant were they not so exact – the rowing movement of the legs suggesting a resemblance to the oars of Ulysses' galley, for instance, and the shell a warrior's shield. The oxymoron, *little Titan* (59), delightfully encapsulates the poem's control over the games it is playing with scale. A further point of comparison is that of tone. In *Snake* it is essentially one of religious awe and utter solemnity. In *Baby Tortoise* the affectionate mock-heroic tone helps to establish the pose of amused empathy with what is playfully assumed to be the creature's life-experience. (For more detailed notes on this poem see p. 122.)

The comparison also raises the question of anthropomorphism in the poems from *Birds, Beasts and Flowers*. The projection of human attributes onto non-human subjects routinely pervades most writing

about animals, even where – as with the rabbits of *Watership Down* –
there is a strong interest in the natural history of the species.
Lawrence betrays little in the way of a naturalist's knowledge of the
creatures he describes. He generally uses direct observation as a
basis for a series of intuitions. *Snake* is evidently more about human
nature than it is about snake nature, but while there are fleeting
anthropomorphic touches – the snake is *like a guest* (28) and *a king*
(68) – the point of the poem turns upon the recognition of the
snake's otherness, its non-humanness, set against which the poet
finds himself lacking. The baby tortoise, in contrast, gradually
acquires a proto-human status, until in *Tortoise Shout* (p. 65),
despite the exactness of the description of his coupling, he is
essentially a stand-in for the human male in an exploration of the
ambivalences of intercourse.

There is nothing intrinsically superior about either approach, of
course, and there is rather more observation of the tortoise's
behaviour than there is of the snake's. It is always worth looking
carefully at the terms on which Lawrence parts from his animals,
having generally learnt something about them and something about
himself. He defers to the snake, is baffled by fish, and swats the
mosquito: inferiority, uncomparability, and superiority. There is a
striking open-mindedness about Lawrence in his animal encounters;
you never quite know what turn his mind will take. Though the
animals generally end up carrying a moral burden, it is rarely a
conventional one, nor one that could have been predicted from the
outset. This imparts a sense of adventure to the poems; the
exhilarating feel of notions living dangerously. The variety of
subjects, tones, moods, ideas, and the exact relationship eventually
established between man and thing exact alert reading. This is true
of the whole range of poems from mock odes, such as *Mosquito*
(p. 44); conversational poems, such as *Peach* (p. 37); acts of
attention such as *Snake* (p. 59); semi-comic performance poems,
such as *Man and Bat* (p. 53); tragi-comic myth making as in the
tortoise poems; creatures seen as natural emblems of their place of
origin, as in *Turkey-Cock* (p. 69) and *Kangaroo* (p. 73) to the bold
religious meditations of *Almond Blossom* (p. 40) and *Medlars and
Sorb-Apples* (p. 38).

Pansies: Fresh Air of Open Consciousness

The poems in this group reveal a variety of ways of expressing passing thoughts. Some of the pieces, and not just or always the longer ones, develop into complete poems – *The Triumph of the Machine* (p. 87) or *Desire is Dead* (p. 86), for example – while many are deliberately fragmentary. The disarmingly modest title, *Pansies*, arises from an intriguing collocation of puns: in French, *pensées* means 'thoughts' and the verb *panser* means 'to dress a wound'. In English, the common name for wild pansies, much smaller and more delicate than the boldly-coloured cultivated varieties, is 'heartsease'. The poems are therefore, self-confessedly, written more often than not as a form of pain-relief. Some of them are innovative, with Lawrence writing directly out of moods, such as irritability, frustration, depression, and even spite, which poetry traditionally sublimates. A few return to rhyme, as in the sprightly doggerel autobiography of *Red-Herring* (p. 84) or the carefully paced sensuousness of *The Elephant is Slow to Mate* (p. 82).

The minimalistic free verse of the majority stems logically from Lawrence's interest in achieving direct utterance from different parts of the self:

> We have roots, and our roots are in the sensual, instinctive and intuitive body, and it is here that we need fresh air of open consciousness.

The honest airing of ill-feeling, as a kind of purge, is as much a part of this process as the nobler and more mysterious flowerings. However, while therapy may be a good reason for someone to write poems, in itself it provides scant reason for anyone else to read them.

Activity

What, if anything, makes *To Women, as Far as I'm Concerned* (p. 85) worth reading?

Discussion

The repeated opening of the first five lines combines a real sense of exasperated insistence with the impression of a devastatingly logical case being built up in stages through a succession of plain statements. The direct address and conversational tone – *you may be pretty sure* (6) – combined with the flat ultimatum delivered in the final line suggest a dramatic attempt to have the final word in a long-lasting argument. The poem memorably and briefly articulates a useful half-truth: true feeling cannot be willed into existence, and talk about feelings often falsifies them. You may find additionally provocative the implication that the poet considers himself the victim of women's will towards emotional dishonesty. You may also find that surprisingly this is a poem you will be able to recall verbatim without ever having set out to learn it.

There is, for all their evident limitations, an air of open honesty wafting from the often tetchy origins of some of the *Pansies*. Equally, there are undercurrents, in the serenity of *Desire is Dead* (p. 86) or the delicate use of classical myth in *For a Moment* (p. 89), of certain qualities in the posthumously published *Last Poems* which are considered on p. 152. The various groupings discussed in this first section are by no means wholly distinct in subject, feeling or form, and in the Tasks on pp. 172–6 other ways of relating the poems across these groupings are suggested.

Approaches Through Lawrence's Life

Lawrence's life, so intimately linked with his writing, has itself taken on the broad symbolic suggestiveness of myth. The Chronology on pp. 167–9 provides key dates and details. In outline the life reveals the origins in personal experience of so many of the dualities which he expressed and theorized about in his work: *for in the tension of opposites all things have their being*, states a prose introduction to *Birds, Beasts and Flowers*. The Nottinghamshire mining country where Lawrence was born and grew up provided the intense juxtapositions of the organic, rural life of the farms with the increasingly mechanized, industrial routines of the pits: *a queer jumble of the old England and the new*. Conflict between his parents, the father a miner – the mother a former school-teacher, set up psychological tensions between a dark, mysterious physical underworld and an everyday, respectable surface world of household tasks and intellectual aspiration. This made a clear contribution to his theory about the rival consciousnesses of the blood and the nerves: the one instinctive and warm, the other will-driven and cold.

The closeness of the bond between Lawrence and his mother, the final rejection of the friend of his youth, Jessie Chambers, and his elopement and eventual marriage with Frieda Weekley (née von Richthofen) – a free-thinking German aristocrat and wife of a professor at Nottingham University College – offer symbolic examples of his different relationships with women. He moved from possessive mother love to spiritual companionship, and eventually to fulfilment through embracing the foreign and other. Lawrence was disillusioned with formal higher education, he trained and worked as a secondary school teacher, and in his satirical writing rejected the country-house literary world of society hostesses and Cambridge professors. These aspects of his character and work contribute to his image as a working-class genius, ill-at-ease in the social circles to which his talents admitted him, nurturing a hostility to social pretension, and to what he saw as the bloodless over-refinement of academic talk.

The openness about sex in Lawrence's work (several of his books and paintings were subject to censorship by publishers or the State) gave him a public notoriety. This served to promote a prophetic image of him but induced in Lawrence himself feelings of rejection and persecution. The First World War of 1914–18 contributed to his personal sense of historical and spiritual crisis and sent his imagination on a utopian quest for *a new heaven and a new earth*. After 1919 he rarely visited England. Travel and residence abroad, in Austria, Italy, Sicily, Australia, and New Mexico combined ideas of exile and pilgrimage. This was a forced rejection of an England that had become cold, mechanical, over-sophisticated and world-weary. It was a search for a fuller existence through encounters with forces of life in the animal kingdom, and through intuitions about the ancient religious customs of warmer countries in which the primitive still seemed accessible. Successive bouts of serious respiratory illness, culminating in death from tuberculosis at the age

151

of forty-five, are reflected in the apparent fascination in his writing with the links between corruption and creativity, death and rebirth.

Knowledge of Lawrence's life, however detailed, does not provide a key to the understanding of a single poem. In outline, however, it does provide a context of associations which enables the poems, even in selection and in the rough order of composition in which they appear here, to express the trajectory of the life. In *Early Poems* the father, the mother, the countryside, and the girl-friend predominate. In *Look! We Have Come Through!* the struggle for balanced relatedness in marriage is portrayed. *Birds, Beasts and Flowers* reveal a roving curiosity in the representative life forms of different places, while the argumentative outbursts against anti-life tendencies in the modern world in *Pansies* display Lawrence's ideas on class-consciousness, mental interference with feelings, money and machine-dominated routines. In *Last Poems*, meditation on gods and spiritual anticipation of death are central. Examples of poems where biographical associations, without providing the main focus for interpretation, convey an additional meaning are *Bavarian Gentians* (p. 97) and *Invocation to the Moon* (p. 96). Is it fanciful to sense Lawrence's collier father behind the descent into the dark subterranean realm of the male deity Pluto, or his mother behind the ascent through the heavens to the house of the moon goddess Aphrodite?

Lawrence himself chose to organize his work in chronological order of writing because:

> many of the poems are so personal that, in their fragmentary
> fashion, they make up a biography of an emotional and inner life.

This can be a rewarding way of reading them providing that the poems are permitted to express their own life. Unlike novels, collections of poetry rarely offer single narratives, and the tendency for readers to try to unify isolated perceptions by stringing them together on a thread of biography is usually reductive.

How then can a reading of Lawrence's poetry respect this closeness between writing and living? *Art for my sake* was his retort to those who preached *art for art's sake*. First, in recognizing that the life the poems record is emotional and inner rather than social, you can look at how Lawrence used his poems as a means of discovering what his feelings were by giving voice to them. This is related to the idea introduced earlier of the demon speaking through the poems so that they:

> seemed to come from somewhere, I didn't quite know where, out of a me whom I didn't know and didn't want to know.
>
> Foreword to *Collected Poems*

Sometimes, as in *Snake* (p. 59), this process is dramatized through a dialogue between contending aspects of the self. But in other poems the interplay between voices or impulses is less schematized.

Secondly, you can explore the extent to which each poem regulates, comments upon, or contains the feelings it expresses. Does the poem, if only in part, achieve control of the feelings or does it surrender to them? And if the poem does surrender to the feelings are they merely expressed by the poet or are they also successfully communicated to a reader?

However, perhaps the fullest response you can offer writing of this kind is to follow Lawrence's advice and bring to it the kind of intelligent, honest intensity he felt readers ought to bring to all art:

> we judge a work of art by its effect on our sincere and vital emotion, and nothing else
>
> Essay on John Galsworthy

– in other words, test the poems against your own experience of life.

This issue of the importance of 'felt life' in Lawrence's poems has been responsible for much criticism that has been influential in swaying opinion against them. In attacking what he called *the fallacy of expressive form*, R. P. Blackmur found Lawrence guilty of believing

> that if a thing is intensely enough felt its mere expression in words will give it satisfactory form; the dogma, in short, that once material becomes words it is its own best form.
>
> *D. H. Lawrence and Expressive Form*

Two lines of defence are possible; the one straightforward, the other more elaborate. First, whilst some of Lawrence's pronouncements do adopt a simplistic opposition between pro-life and pro-form tendencies in poets (*the desire for chaos is the breath of their poetry. The fear of chaos is in their parade of forms and technique*) he actually comes closest to a formless flatness of utterance in the *Pansies*, few of which originate in intense emotional states. In fact, he rewrote and revised much of his work and most of the poems in this collection are achieved wholes in their different forms.

The second line of defence involves a partial concession to the criticism. Lawrence does indeed make a show of artlessness in much of his poetry. He seeks naïvety of perception and expression, and rejects the idea that art has a value in itself. Many of Lawrence's early twentieth-century poetic contemporaries, T. S. Eliot, Ezra Pound and W. B. Yeats, for example, sought for perfection of form in their poems to provide a compensatory victory over the formlessness, or at least the imperfections, of life. Lawrence, in contrast, generally resisted the allure of the idea of the compensatory value of perfected form as an end in itself, and aimed for a looseness of expression which at times might make for slipshod writing but at others, it let life in.

Approaches Through Lawrence's Ideas

Religion

There was much irreverence in Lawrence's attitude to established religions. The Bhudda and Jesus, he felt, were *utter pessimists as regards life, teaching that the only happiness lay in abstracting oneself from life...* Nevertheless, the way Lawrence looked at life was essentially religious. Attendance at the Congregational Chapel in Eastwood made him aware of the power of language to arouse feelings of awe. *The hymns which I learned as a child*, he later asserted, *...mean more to me than the finest poetry*. The rhythms, cadences and imagery of the Bible were a major influence on his style of writing, and they inform the configurations of this thought. Taken as a whole, his work might be seen as a series of attempts to articulate a personal religion with its own psalms, hymns, parables, myths and the occasional sermon. In reading the poems, you may be aware intermittently that you are being urged to share a faith. But in what?

His central beliefs arise from a conviction that the universe is an expression of a life-force which is inherently meaningful. The question of existence, then, is less a search for meaning but rather an alertness to the ebb and flow of the life-force in oneself and of its quickening through revelatory contact with other living things. A sense of significant pattern arises from the seasonal cycle of new life, fruition, death, decay, and rebirth, and the influences of the sun and the moon. Daily life itself becomes a potential religious experience, and writing a kind of devotional discipline undertaken in a spirit of spontaneous attentiveness rather than out of sober duty. 'Birds, Beasts and Flowers' (the phrase is taken from *Now the Day is Over*, a popular hymn) are interpretations of the life-force and are themselves given the status of religious objects, perhaps with souls and gods of their own. Indeed, they are capable of inspiring the *wonder* which Lawrence came to regard as the *natural religious sense*:

> Plant consciousness, insect consciousness, fish consciousness, are all related by one permanent element, which we may call the religious element inherent in all life, even in a flea: the sense of wonder.
>
> *Hymns in a Man's Life*

The bearing of this comment upon the poems of *Birds, Beasts and Flowers* is obvious; what it does not bring out is the way these poems interweave the wonder with a frequently irreverent playfulness and sometimes with honest bathos, which serves to undermine over-elevated assumptions. Any tendency towards disproportionate solemnity is upset as the creatures overturn or frustrate the poet's designs upon them. Lawrence rather liked the way in which actual experiences were inclined to demand flexible theories. *The Man of Tyre* (p. 93) provides an example of this, and many of the animal poems enact it.

Activity

One Lawrentian theory about contact with animals was as follows:

> The primary way, in our existence, to get vitality is to absorb it from living creatures lower than ourselves. It is thus transformed into a new and higher creation. (There are many ways of absorbing:

devouring food is one way, love is often another. The best way is a pure relationship, which includes the being on each side, and which allows the transfer to take place in a living flow, enhancing the life in both beings.)

Hymns in a Man's Life

To what extent do the poems bear out or resist this theory?

Discussion

You may find yourself wondering what the kangaroo or the fish take away from their contact with Lawrence. In fact, this is just the sort of comic self-deflation some of the poems go in for: the superiority of the snake in its poised selfhood, the limited awareness of the fish for whom Lawrence is a monster, the triumphant escape of the bat, the ambiguous status of the turkey-cock. The wonder inspired is not always a matter of awe; equally often it is a kind of spirited, playful curiosity. Underlying the *Birds, Beasts and Flowers* poems, one senses a fragmentary religious theory of natural types which never fully came into being. The animals and plants, in their particularity, put up stern resistance.

Sex

Lawrence's ideas about sex can be seen most clearly in the context of his 'religious' thought. The most powerful manifestation of the life-force is a creature's sexual feelings: attraction, repulsion, desire, and tenderness. Intercourse renews the life-force, not only through the possibility of creating offspring, but also in being the most intense and intimate way of exchanging vitality in a living flow. This, rather than prurience, accounts for the number of poems about sex between animals as well as between humans. It also helps to explain the religious character of many of the poems about sex. You might look, for example, at the awed sense of participation in a profound ritual in *The Chief Mystery* (p. 24), or the glorious involvement of angels in the love-making in *Whales Weep Not!* (p. 94).

The individual's experience of intercourse is complicated by a paradox, however: the fact of the incompleteness of the individual – as man or woman, male or female – is implicit in the act of sexual union. In sex, awareness of the individual's lack of completeness is experienced intensely, close to the moment of fulfilment. The sex act brings men and women up against this frightening contradiction: hence Lawrence's compensatory emphasis on the need for a sense of balance which is established in but transcends the moment of climax – *sex is the balance of male and female in the universe* – and on the life-enhancing view that in sex one temporarily loses one's sense of self (this is clearly exemplified in *The Chief Mystery* p. 24) in order to renew it, to feel confirmed and 'balanced'. This state is perhaps best conveyed in the unmistakably post-coital *Roses On the Breakfast Table* (p.28). The paradox of sex takes on a tragic and no less religious form in the identification Lawrence establishes between intercourse and the crucifixion of Christ or the dismemberment of Osiris. Sex can be experienced as an anguished tearing apart of the self, a death, from which a new life may emerge. Lawrence often lamented the church's tendency to idolize images of the Madonna and Child and the Crucifixion to the exclusion of his own favourite image of Christ risen in the flesh, living his life as a man beyond the cross. The whole dilemma over sex helps to explain the curious combination of pity and envy felt for the fish, which does not need to meet its mate to reproduce.

Two further points deserve mention here. First, Lawrence felt that in the modern world sex had become *bloodless*, an affair of the mind and the nerves, compulsive but unsatisfying. Hence his appreciation of the full-blooded, rhythmic and patiently achieved unions of the whales and elephants. Hence, also the attacks in *Pansies* upon various forms of what he often called *sex-in-the-head*, an obsessive interest in achieving shallow gratification without the full consent of the body.

True sexuality requires the acceptance that periods of impotence, as in *Desire is Dead* (p. 86), form part of a natural cycle. For:

sex goes through the rhythm of the year, in man and woman, ceaselessly changing: the rhythm of the sun in relation to the earth.

Reflections on the Death of a Porcupine

The *Look! We Have Come Through!* sequence traces the struggle for equilibrium between man and woman in marriage through different phases: the desire for balance frustrated by a lingering sense of vulnerability in *Bei Hennef* (p. 26); the tender appreciation of the woman unbroken by any immediate desire to possess in *Gloire de Dijon* (p. 28); the conviction that the life-force, imaged as a fountain welling up from within, is blessing the relationship in *Song of a Man Who Has Come Through* (p. 31); and the desire for personal fulfilment to be accompanied by a seasonal, historical, even cosmic renewal in *Craving for Spring* (p. 32).

The second point worth discussing may arise from the reader's response to the roles that Lawrence assigns men and women in his poems. Women readers are drawn to Lawrence by his obvious interest in writing about women's experiences, but are often left feeling uneasy about his attitudes. The openness of his writing about sex has provided a focus for feminist criticism. Starting from the view that literature in general not only reflects but also tends to reinforce men's dominance over women, such criticism sets out to challenge male supremacy by examining the ways in which gender roles are represented.

Activity

Make your own assessment of Lawrence's portrayal of women. To make a start you might look at the characteristics he attributes to mothers, girl-friends, lovers, wives and goddesses. In which poems and in what ways are women seen as superior, as inferior, or as equal to men? Are they viewed with admiration, desire, tenderness, hostility, or with some combination of these? What significance would you attach to Lawrence's frequent decision to write from a female viewpoint?

Discussion

Feminist criticism of Lawrence's writing divides into two main strands of argument. On the one hand, he often shows women gaining fulfilment through a yielding acceptance of masculine dominance in sex. Many of the heroines in his novels and stories, for example Ursula in *Women in Love*, do indeed set out to seize the initiative, only to succumb, eventually, to the phallic power of the hero. On this type of reading, for which it is easy to find evidence, Lawrence is branded a supreme example of a male chauvinist. However, his treatment of gender can be seen as more searching than this. Lawrence's writing frequently alternates between male and female points of view, and in doing so, gives a more ambiguous and complex account of what men and women do, feel, and want, than just a list of examples of male supremacy would suggest. You may find much sympathetic identification with women characters caught in between the wish to revere and the desire to subject and control.

These two arguments can be further put to the test by a closer study of particular poems in which the experience of sex is viewed from male and female perspectives.

Activity

Read *Cruelty and Love* (p. 4), *Ballad of Another Ophelia* (p. 22), *The Chief Mystery* (p. 24), and *A Young Wife* (p. 27). What differences do you find between these in the presentation of men's and women's experience of love?

Discussion

You may find that *Cruelty and Love* strikes the key note in its title. The man is shown as a natural aggressor and the woman as a fearful but ultimately compliant victim. Three of these poems are rendered through the woman's point of view and in each case the tendency is to glorify the man's power which is seen in contradictory terms: dark/sun-like, dangerous/attractive, predatory/life-enhancing. Sex and death are closely identified. There is an unmistakable celebration of a dominant masculine power here. You may, however, find it significant that whilst the woman in *Cruelty and Love* finds *death good*, the experiences of the young wife, and in particular Ophelia, are much more ambivalent. It is fair to observe, also, that the one poem written from the man's viewpoint, *The Chief Mystery*, is quite frank about his feelings of vulnerability and fear. You can see this focus intensified in a later poem like *Tortoise Shout* (p. 65).

Revealingly, it is the poems imagined from the female point of view that tend to glorify male potency and in which, arguably, an element of wishful projection persists. Might the experiences of women, as

imagined by Lawrence in these poems, combine a personal understanding of what it is like to feel vulnerable with an attempt to allay
male fears of inadequacy, i.e. by an over-insistence on women's
sensitivity and ultimate acknowledgement of the power of men? See
the Notes for a more detailed discussion of these individual poems.

Thinking

Two of the poems in this selection are explicitly about Lawrence's
preferred ways of thinking: *Thought* (p. 90) and *Relativity* (p. 87).
The fact that they are both *Pansies* is no accident since the very
title of the collection is a pun on *pensées*, French for thoughts. The
title is specifically associated with the philosopher Pascal whose
Pensées offered a fragmentary and uncompleted defence of
Christianity. Lawrence clearly conceived of his *Pansies* as a low-key,
and equally fragmentary, defence of his own habits of thought.
Lawrence felt that a thought was different from an *idea or an opinion
or a didactic statement*: it was an act linked to the moment of
utterance coming *as much from the heart and the genitals as from the
head*: impulsive, intuitional, passing. He preferred to write them in
poetry, or rather not in prose, because it made them seem less
premeditated. You may feel that this notion can be countered in
practice by our cultural expectation that the language of poetry
should bear more close attention than that of prose. The very high
value placed on actual or apparent spontaneity of thought in
Lawrence's writing arises from his conviction that true thought is
not an affair of the mind alone but of *man in his wholeness wholly
attending*, and so involves the blood and the body. An attempt to
define the type of thought he was after led to the concept of the
emotional mind:

> Now the emotional mind... is not logical. It is a psychological fact,
> that when we are thinking emotionally or passionately, thinking and
> feeling at the same time, we do not think rationally: and therefore,
> and therefore, and therefore. Instead, the mind makes curious
> swoops and circles. It touches upon the point of pain or interest,
> then, sweeps away again in a cycle, coils round and approaches
> again the point of pain or interest. There is a curious spiral rhythm,
> and the mind approaches again and again the point of concern...

n there, down there
vn the blue depths of mountain gentian flowers
d, cold
e gathering to a wedding in the [winter] dark
own the dark blue path

Vhat a dark-blue gloom   20
f gentians here in the sunny room!

avarian Gentians

Not every man has gentians in his house
In soft September, at slow, sad Michaelmas.
Bavarian gentians, tall and dark, but dark
darkening the daytime torch-like with the smoking blueness of
     Pluto's gloom,
ribbed hellish flowers erect, with their blaze of darkness spread blue,
blown flat into points, by the heavy white draught of the day.

Torch-flowers of the blue-smoking darkness, Pluto's dark-blue blaze
black lamps from the halls of Dis, smoking dark blue
giving off darkness, blue darkness, upon Demeter's yellow-pale
     day
whom have you come for, here in the white-cast day?   10

Reach me a gentian, give me a torch!
let me guide myself with the blue, forked torch of a flower
down the darker and darker stairs, where blue is darkened on
     blueness
down the way Persephone goes, just now, in first-frosted
     September,
to the sightless realm where darkness is married to dark
and Persephone herself is but a voice, as a bride,
a gloom invisible enfolded in the deeper dark
of the arms of Pluto as he ravishes her once again
and pierces her once more with his passion of the utter dark
among the splendour of black-blue torches, shedding fathomless
     darkness on the nuptials.

Give me a flower on a tall stem, and three dark flames,
for I will go to the wedding, and be wedding-guest
at the marriage of the living dark.

until at last there is the closing in, and the clutch of a decision or a
resolve.

Preface to *Cavalleria Rusticana*

This passage quoted at length, illustrates Lawrence's tendency to use the rhythms of his language to exemplify what he describes. This is a characteristic of many of this poems. It is also a defence of the frequent repetitions of words and phrases in his poems. However, this style carries with it dangers as well as its own appeal. It might easily be used to argue that Lawrence's work is inarticulate or tautological. Equally it raises the issue of whether poems should reproduce acts of thought in something like their entirety or whether they should be the polished products of much effort. Many of the formal tensions and so of the critical questions posed by Lawrence's poetry arise from this contradiction. The valuing of process over product can indeed result in a lot of bad art. Lawrence's work is often pulled between a desire to remain faithful to the actual experience of its composition and the need to find a form which communicates an experience in a more concentrated form and so objectifies it.

Symbol and Myth

Through symbol and myth can be found a way of thinking which admits a sense of wonder and allows emotions to work closely with the mind. This is why they are a feature of much religious writing. They are focused rather than diffuse ways of engaging the *emotional mind*, and expressing shifting responses to the mysteries of life. For Lawrence:

Myth is an attempt to narrate a whole human experience, of which the purpose is too deep, going too deep in the blood and soul, for mental explanation or description… And the images of myths are symbols.

Introduction to *The Dragon of the Apocalypse*

Stemming from Lawrence's emphasis on the divinity of the natural, his poetry is pervaded by images which are organic – trees, flowers; elemental – earth, wind, water and fire; cosmic – the sun and the moon; as well as by symbolic borrowings from Christian and classical myth: the crucifixion, Persephone and Pluto, Osiris and Isis and Dionysos. Allusions to specific myths are explained in the notes to specific poems. A broader perspective on these symbols can be gained by looking at how they inform Lawrence's modes of thought across the range of his poems.

Activity

What uses does Lawrence make of the symbol of the tree in his poetry?

Discussion

The tree symbol has a dual origin: as a naturally occurring instance of noble organic growth, and as a religious symbol – the biblical Tree of Life which grew in the Garden of Eden. Lawrence generates through the tree a set of images of life seen as a natural process with religious significance: roots, blossoms, fruits, seasonal changes. Individual poems show close observation to the figurative possibilities of a particular species (*Almond Blossom* p. 40). He also uses the tree to provide a parallel for a human drama (*Discord in Childhood* p. 1) or to offer consolation through an analogy between human life and tree life (*Desire is Dead* p. 86).

Thinking in symbols can lead to the reworking of old myths. Perhaps the finest example of this in Lawrence's poems is *Bavarian Gentians* which is the focus of the concluding section.

Approaches Through the Single Poem

The existence of two earlier versions of *Bavarian Gentians* provides an opportunity to trace the development of the poem from original idea to Lawrence's preferred version.

Activity

Study the two versions of *Glory of Darkness* and the penultimate version of *Bavarian Gentians* given below. Compare them with the final version on p. 97. In what ways does Lawrence improve the

poem by redrafting? Is there any image, phra[...] in the penultimate version that you feel the fina[...]

Glory of Darkness
[Ink version:]

    Blue and dark
    Oh Bavarian gentians, tall ones
    make a dark-blue gloom
    in the sunny room.

    They have added blueness to blueness, until
    it is dark: beauty
    blue joy of my soul
    Bavarian gentians
    your dark blue gloom is so noble!

    How deep I have gone   10
    dark gentians
    since I embarked on your dark blue fringes
    how deep, how deep, how happy!
    What a journey for my soul
    in the blue dark gloom
    of gentians here in the sunny room!

Glory of Darkness
[Pencil version:]

    ....
    it is dark
    and the door is open
    to the depths.

    It is so blue, it is so dark
    in the dark doorway
    and the way is open
    to Hades.

    Oh, I know—
    Persephone has just gone back
    down the thickening thickening gloom   10
    of dark-blue gentians to Pluto
    to her bridegroom in the dark
    and all the dead
    and all the dark great ones of the underworld

Discussion

The first draft of *Glory of Darkness* arises from an observed contrast between sunlight and the dark blue gloom of the gentians. It appears that contemplation of the flowers has induced a period of oblivion which is figured in the poem as a vague journey of the soul. The rhythm, however, has little to do with the experience; the poem is a set of exclamations which refer but do not enact. The pencil version reveals the mythical destination and with it the idea of the wedding. It begins to move in a slow descending cadence until brought up short by the glib chiming of the final two lines.

In the penultimate version a more precise observation of the characteristics of the flower gives rise naturally to a full integration of metaphor, action, and myth. The opening is now poised and arresting as the spontaneous sense of being special in the first line nicely gives onto the melancholy autumnal undertow of the second. There remains, however, an inappropriate wordiness in places — *black-blue... fathomless... nuptials* (20) — which intrudes fussily upon the prevailing movement of descent. There is also a jarringly histrionic excitement in the description of the ravishment of Persephone by Pluto, and a slight lapse into Lawrentian sexual jargon in the phrase *passion of the utter dark* (19). In the final poem there is a sonorous mysteriousness about the union. Do you find the equivalent passage, *pierced with the passion of dense gloom* (19), imaginatively closer to the emotional perspective of Persephone and the guest than it is to that of Pluto?

It is, perhaps, a pity that the final poem dispensed with its predecessor's last three lines. They express a dignified resolve to participate in the ultimate ceremony. But does the poem gain from what is a distancing withdrawal from the darkness which has already imaginatively consumed bride, groom, and guest? Is not the idea, in the final version, that the poet is essentially a follower in the footsteps of Persephone, rather than the more detached wedding guest who participates only through observation, a richer one? The replacing of the merely physical *arms of Pluto* (18) in the penultimate version with the grandly heraldic *arms Plutonic* (18) adds to the tendency of the final poem towards a richer suggestiveness.

In the vanishing image of its close, the last version finally lays the ghost of the crude rhyme which ended the first attempt and achieves a haunting, echoing sonority of phrase. The poem succeeds in bringing together precise observation, originality of metaphor, the reworking of myth, and the idea that there is in death a possibility of renewal, in a free verse which projects the poet's meditative mood. For these reasons *Bavarian Gentians* is often held up as the consummation of Lawrence's work as a poet.

Chronology

1885   Lawrence born on 11 September, one of five children, in Eastwood, Nottinghamshire. His father was a miner, his mother Lydia Beardsall was a schoolteacher before her marriage

1887   Queen Victoria's Jubilee

1891   Thomas Hardy, *Tess of The D'Urbervilles*

1892   Death of Tennyson, Poet Laureate

1898   Wins scholarship to Nottingham High School

1899   Outbreak of Boer War

1901   Becomes a clerk at surgical appliance factory; seriously ill with pneumonia; elder brother Ernest dies; meets Jessie Chambers, intellectual companion and first love.
Death of Queen Victoria

1902   Starts work as pupil teacher in Eastwood.
Joseph Conrad, *Heart of Darkness*

1903   Wright brothers make first successful aeroplane flight

1905   Begins to write poetry.
Einstein proposes theory of relativity

1906   Enrols on teacher-training course at Nottingham University College; begins *The White Peacock*, his first novel

1908   Becomes teacher in a Croydon Secondary School.
Introduction of old age pensions

1909   *The English Review* publishes some of Lawrence's poems

1910   Death of mother; begins *Sons and Lovers*.
Death of Edward VII, accession of George V; E. M. Forster, *Howards End*

1911   *The White Peacock* published

1912   Leaves teaching. Travels in Europe with Frieda Weekley. *Titanic* sinks on maiden voyage; *Georgian Poetry* (Anthology); Ezra Pound, *Ripostes* (poems)

1913   *Sons and Lovers* and some early poems published

1914   Returns to England and marries Frieda. Outbreak of First World War; Imagist anthology of poetry

1915   *The Rainbow* published but considered indecent; publishers prosecuted and copies destroyed

1916   Lawrence declared unfit for military service. James Joyce, *Portrait of the Artist as a Young Man*

1917   Lawrence and Frieda expelled from Cornwall as suspected spies; *Look! We Have Come Through!* published. Bolshevik Revolution in Russia

1918   *New Poems* published. End of First World War; Women (aged 30 and over) granted the vote

1919   Lives in Italy – rarely returns to England after this

1920   *Women in Love* published; living in Sicily. W. B. Yeats, *Michael Robartes and the Dancer* (poems)

1921   *Sea and Sardinia*, a travel book, published

1922   Visits Ceylon, Australia, and California before settling on a ranch near Taos, New Mexico. T. S. Eliot, *The Waste Land*

1923   Death of father; *Birds, Beasts and Flowers* published

1924   First Labour Government elected

1926   Begins *Lady Chatterley's Lover*; settles near Florence, Italy; last visit to England. General Strike.